Carl Robert Osten-Sacken

Enumeration of the Diptera of the Malayan Archipelago

Carl Robert Osten-Sacken

Enumeration of the Diptera of the Malayan Archipelago

ISBN/EAN: 9783741130403

Manufactured in Europe, USA, Canada, Australia, Japa

Cover: Foto ©Thomas Meinert / pixelio.de

Manufactured and distributed by brebook publishing software
(www.brebook.com)

Carl Robert Osten-Sacken

Enumeration of the Diptera of the Malayan Archipelago

ENUMERATION

OF THE DIPTERA OF THE MALAY ARCHIPELAGO

COLLECTED

by Prof. ODOARDO BECCARI, M.ʳ L. M. D'ALBERTIS and others

by C. R. OSTEN SACKEN

PREFACE

The insects which form the subject of the present paper, were collected by Prof. Odoardo Beccari, principally in Celebes, Ternate, Amboina, New Guinea, the Aru Islands (1873-75), and in Sumatra (1878); by M.ʳ L. M. D'Albertis in New Guinea (1872 and 1876-77) and by M.ʳ G. B. Ferrari in Java (1875). They belong to the Museo Civico in Genoa.

In accepting the flattering proposal of the authorities of the Museo Civico to describe this collection, I undertook a task which was somewhat above my level, as my dipterological studies had hitherto been confined to North American diptera, and especially to a limited number of families of that order. However, I have been able to compensate in a measure my deficiencies in knowledge and experience, by means of the facilities for travelling, which I enjoy, and which enabled me to compare the types of a large number of the species I had to name.

A work like the present must, of necessity, be considered as only preliminary, preparing materials for monographic work. For this reason, I did not deem it my duty to describe as new, every specimen that I could not determine. The effect of this kind of pseudo-conscientiousness merely is, to add to the mass of scientific rubbish of *species dubiae* with which dipterology is more afflicted than any other branch of entomology ([1]). It is not urgent at all, to describe every single species of exotic *Sciara*, *Culex*, *Anthomyia* etc., the more so as the european species of these genera are as yet insufficiently known. Even the detailed working out of such genera as (in the present instance) *Tabanus*, *Ommatius*, *Maira*, *Psilopus* etc., must be left to the monographer. M.[r] van der Wulp has made an excellent beginning with his monograph of the Asilidae of the Archipelago. And the opportunities for such monographic treatment would become more frequent, if the public museums, imitating the noble example of the Museo Civico of Genoa, adopted a more liberal policy in communicating their materials to the would-be monographer. Such lists as the present would, in such a case serve to show, where the materials are to be found.

In concluding, I take pleasure to express my sincere gratitude to the authorities of the British Museum and of the Zoological Museums in Vienna and Leiden, and also to M.[r] v. d. Wulp, at the Hague for the facilities which they have offered me during the preparation of this work. I am greatly indebted to D.[r] Gestro, Vice Director of the Museo Civico, for his unfailing kindness and assistance. The admirable order in which I received the collections, especially as to the labeling with localities and dates, has greatly facilitated the progress of my work.

Florence, Novemb. 1880.

Ch. R. OSTEN SACKEN.

([1]) The extent to which this last statement is true will become clear to those who will take the trouble to read the Preface to my: Catalogue of the described Diptera of North-America, second edition, Washington 1878.

EXPLANATIONS.

With each species, I have quoted the *principal* description only.

An *exclamation* (!) after a quotation, means that I have seen the type of the species. The types of Doleschall I have compared in the Museum in Vienna.

Among several conflicting names, I have given preference to the one, whose identification seemed the most probable.

Synonymics borrowed from other works are followed by the authority in brackets.

MYCETOPHILIDAE.

Sciara sp. — One ♀, Kandari, Celebes, April 1874 *(Beccari)*. Its red thoracic dorsum seems to mimic a *Plecia*.

Sciara sp. — 2 ♀, Hatam, N. Guinea, June 1875 *(Beccari)*.

Sciara sp. — 2 ♀, Aru Islds., Wokan, 1873 *(Beccari)*.

Mycetophila sp. — One specim. Kandari, Celebes, April 1874 *(Beccari)*. Has a good deal of *Myc. obscurata* Wk. (Salwatty). Its compressed thorax and large fore coxae (as long as the fore femora), give it a peculiar appearance.

BIBIONIDAE.

Bibio obediens n. sp. ♀. Reddish-yellow, including the coxae and femora; antennae (except the base), tibiae and tarsi black; wings brownish, costal margin darker. Long. corp. 9 mm.

Palpi and lips blackish; antennae deep-black, except the scapus, which is yellow; ocellar tubercle black; tibiae and tarsi black, shining. The rest of the body, including halteres, coxae and femora, reddish-yellow. Thoracic dorsum with a semi-appressed fulvous pubescence. The outer spine of the front tibiae at least twice as long and much stronger, than the inner one; they are dark reddish-brown. Wings brownish, darker along the anterior margin; this darker tinge fills out the costal, anterior basal and marginal cells, and invades the anterior portion of the first posterior cell, reaching along the third vein, nearly as far as the tip of the wing; but the interval between the auxiliary and the first veins is much paler; the stigma is represented by a yellowish streak; the second posterior cell is sessile.

Hab. Hatam, New Guinea *(Beccari,* July 1875); a single female.

NB. Resembles *ruficoxis* Macq. and *substituta* Wk., but is easily distinguished by its red femora.

Bibio plecioides n. sp. ♀. Body and legs (including coxae) black; thorax yellowish-red; wings dark brown. Long. corp. 6-7 mm.

Coloring of *Plecia fulvicollis;* head, including antennae; legs, including coxae, and abdomen black; the latter opaque, the head shining: knob of halteres brown, the stem paler. Thorax altogether of a pale reddish-yellow, densely beset on the dorsum with a fine, short, golden-yellow pubescence. The outer spine of the front tibiae nearly three times as long, and much stronger, than the inner one. Wings brown, darker along the costa; stigma dark brown; second posterior cell sessile; the extreme root of the wings is tinged with reddish-yellow.

Hab. Hatam, N. Guinea, July 1875 *(Beccari);* two females.

NB. The short description of *Bibio bicolor* Walker, List etc. 1, 121 (East-Indies) might be identified with this species, nevertheless that species is different; unfortunately I lost the notice containing the statement of the difference, which I took in the Brit. Mus.

I venture to describe this species and the preceding, although I have only females, for the reason that the fauna of the Archipelago does not seem to abound in species of *Bibio*, and thus the two species may be easily recognisable.

Dilophus n. sp. One ♀, Java, 1875 *(Beccari)*. This is the first *Dilophus* from the Malay Archipelago mentioned in print, as far as I know.

Plecia fulvicollis (Fab.) Wied. Auss. Zw. I, 73 (Sumatra, Java). Many specimens from Ternate and Celebes *(Beccari)*, Island Yule, N. Guinea *(L. M. D'Albertis)*.

SYN. **Plecia dorsalis** Walk. J. Pr. Linn. Soc. I, 5 (Singapore).

Plecia tergorata Rondani, Ann. Mus. Civ. etc. 1875, VII., 462 (Borneo). 4♂, 1♀; Tcibodas Ott., Java, Beccari, 1874.

Resembles the preceding very much, but only the thoracic dorsum, including scutellum, are reddish; collare, pleurae, pectus and metathorax are black; root of the wings black.

Plecia melanaspis Wied. Auss. Zw. I, 72 (Java); [*Penthetria* in Wied.].

One ♂, two ♀, Java, 1874 *(Beccari)*.

SYN. **Penthetria Japonica** Wied. Auss. Zw. II, 618 [Loew, Berl. Ent. Z. II, 106].
Penthetria ignicollis Walk. List etc. I, 116; Canton, Nepaul.
Crapitula Motschulskii Gimmerth. Bull. de Moscou, 1845, Eastern Siberia.

Loew, l. c., gives the latter synonymy as probable; he says that. *Crap. Motch.* occurs in the greater part of Asia and also in Europ. Russia.

Plecia forcipata n. sp. — Eleven ♂; Kaju Tanam, Sumatra; Aug. and Sept. 1878 *(Beccari)*.

Resembles *P. fulvicollis* and *tergorata,* but is smaller (7-8 mm.) and holds the middle between both in the coloration of the thorax. Thoracic dorsum red, including the scutellum and meta-notum; pleurae and pectus black; but a broad red stripe rea-

ches from the foot of the halteres, across a portion of the
pleurae and the pectus, between the front and middle coxae and
thus reaches the corresponding point on the opposite side. When
the head in broken off, it becomes apparent that the part of
the thorax against which it is applied, (front part of the collare), is also black (it is red in *P. fulvicollis*). The head is,
proportionally, much smaller than in *P. fulvicollis*, the legs
shorter, the wings comparatively shorter and much narrower;
they are not tinged with reddish at the root; the anterior branch
of the fork of the third vein is a little more oblique and therefore a trifle longer. The valves of the forceps of the male are
much larger than in *P. fulvicollis*, and, in all my (dry) specimens, gaping.

The four species of *Plecia*, enumerated above, and so much
alike in coloring, may be tabulated thus:

> **I.** The anterior branch of the third vein originates near the small
> crossvein, and runs alongside the posterior branch: body
> black, the disc of the thorax alone, more or less reddish . *melanaspis.*
> **II.** The anterior branch of the third vein originates a long distance
> beyond the small crossvein, and is short and oblique.
>   **A.** The thorax is altogether red (including scutellum, meta-
>   notum ad pectus); root of the wings reddish . . . . *fulvicollis.*
>   **AA.** Some portions of the thorax are black; root of the
>   wings brown.
>   *a.* Collare, pleurae, pectus and metanotum black . . . *tergorata.*
>   *aa.* Metanotum red; pleurae and pectus black, except a broad
>   red stripe which extends from the foot of the halteres,
>   across the pectus . . . . *forcipata.*

Plecia sp. — One ♂, Hatam, N. Guin. July 1875 *(Beccari).*
A small, brownish species; thoracic dorsum with darker
stripes.

CULICIDAE.

Megarrhina sp. One ♀; Kandari, Celebes, April 1874 *(Beccari).*
Has a good deal of *M. subulifer* Dol. (♀ of *Amboinensis*
Dol.), but the fringe of hair at the end of the abdomen, on
both sides is yellowish-orange, and not black. Is likewise different from *M. immisericors* Wk., of which I have seen the type.

Megarrhina sp. Two ♂; Ternate 1875 *(Beccari)*.

Megarrhina sp. One ♀; Isl.ᵈ Aru, Wokan 1873 *(Beccari)*.

Culex sp. Ternate; Kandari, Celebes *(Beccari)*.

TIPULIDAE.

Megistocera fuscana Wied. Auss. Zw. I, 55 (Java).
One ♂; Kandari, Celebes, April 1874 *(Beccari);* occurs also in Sumatra (Br. Mus.) and on the Aru Islands (Walker).

Ctenophora gaudens Walk. J. Pr. Linn. Soc. IV, 93 *(Celebes)*.
One ♂; two ♀; Kandari, Celebes, April 1874 *(Beccari)*.
The female differs from the male in the abdomen being velvet-black (and not red) and in the crossband on the wings being interrupted before reaching the posterior margin.

Tipula praepotens Wied. Auss. Zw. I, 40 (Java).
One ♂; Mt. Singalang, Sumatra, July 1878 *(Beccari)*.
This species has a wide distribution, and according to Snellen v. Vollenhoven, occurs even in Japan.

Tipula umbrina Wied. Auss. Zw. I, 49 (Java); comp. also v. d. Wulp. Tijdschr. etc. XXIII.
♂ ♀, Java 1874 *(Beccari)*.

Pachyrrhina Doleschalli (nomen novum).

SYN. **Pachyrrhina javensis** Dolesch. I Bijdr. Tab. 3, f. 1 (Java).
(?) **Pachyrrhina fasciata** Macq. H. N. Dipt. I, 90 (Java).

Two ♀; Buitenzorg, Java, *(Ferrari);* Ajer Mantcior, Sumatra, Aug. 1878 *(Beccari)*.
The figure in Doleschall leaves no doubt about the identity of the species, although the short description contains some

doubtful points. Macquart calls the fifth abdominal segment and the metanotum altogether yellow, which does not agree with my specimens. The specimen from Java has the abdominal black incisures narrower and some other differences too slight to be taken in consideration. I also possess ♂ and ♀ specimens from Ceylon, which I consider to be the same species. As there is an earlier *Pachyrrh. javana* Wied. and as *Tip. fasciata* Degeer is a *Pachyrrhina*, both names should be dropped and the species called *P. Doleschalli.* I give a more complete description of it.

P. Doleschalli (Syn. *P. javensis* Dol.) ♂♀. Orange-yellow; abdominal segments 2-5 have black posterior margins; segments 1, 6 and 7 black; genitals yellow. Length: 12-13 mm.

♂♀ Antennae: two basal joints yellow; the rest black; joints of flagellum, in the male, of the usual, reniform shape. Head yellowish orange; a small black triangle on the occiput; rostrum yellow, a short brownish stripe does not reach its basis, but covers the nasus. Thorax yellow; the usual stripes black, shining; the lateral ones not incurved at tip; scutellum black; metanotum on its posterior margin, with a transverse black spot; pleurae with three more or less dark brown spots under the root of the wings; one of them is linear; sides of the collare black; the middle, yellow. Abdomen yellowish-orange; segment first black above; segments 2-5 with the posterior margins black; segments 6 and 7 black; genitals yellow. Knob of halteres yellow, stem brown. Legs brownish-yellow; knees and tarsi darker. Wings subhyaline; stigma pale brown; discal cell small; second posterior coarctate at base.

Hab. Java, Sumatra, Ceylon.

NB. The spots on the pleurae vary in intensity; in the ♀ from Ceylon only one is visible. In some specimens a brown or reddish spot is visible above the middle coxae; also on the root of the front coxae. The breadth of the abdominal black crossbands is variable. In the ♀ from Ceylon the segments 6 and 7 have some yellow anteriorly.

Pachyrrhina familiaris n. sp. ♂♀. Rostrum and palpi black, abdomen of the ♀ unicolorous, yellow; in the ♂ blackish at the tip only; stigma pale brownish. Long. corp. ♀ 12-13 mm.; ♂ 9-10 mm.

Female. Yellowish-orange; antennae black, of moderate length, two basal joints yellow; rostrum and palpi black; a small, brownish, opaque, triangular spot on the vertex, sometimes hardly perceptible. The usual black thoracic stripes have a grayish lustre; the intermediate one is wedge-shaped, evanescent in front, before reaching the collare, abbreviated before the suture behind. Scutellum and metanotum uniformly yellow; halteres yellow, the knob infuscated. Abdomen yellowish-orange. Legs brownish, femora paler at the base. Wings subhyaline, stigma very pale brownish; discal cell rather small and narrow; second posterior cell sometimes short-petiolate, sometimes subsessile.

Male. Resembles the female, only the antennae are a little longer, the joints of the flagellum are stouter and distinctly coarctate in the middle; there is a more distinct black spot on the vertex; the intermediate thoracic stripe fully reaches the suture before the collare; the scutellum, as well as the posterior margin of the metanotum are somewhat tinged with brownish; the three last abdominal segments are dark brown, but the genitals are yellowish; the stigma is darker brownish.

Four ♀, one ♂; Mt. Singalang, Sumatra, July 1878 *(Beccari)*.

NB. I have no doubt that the male belongs to the same species, the slight difference in coloring notwithstanding. All the specimens are injured from having been kept in spirits.

Pachyrrhina melanura n. sp. ♀. Yellowish-orange; four last abdominal segments black. Length: 13-14 mm.

Head of a saturate yellowish-red (orange), opaque; front very gibbose; antennae black, except the scapus, which is yellowish-orange; palpi brown, more reddish towards the base. Thoracic stripes represented by three wedgeshaped, contiguous, velvet-black spots; the intermediate one bears, in the middle, a smooth, shining spot, likewise black, and having the shape of a narrow arrowhead, whose point is truncate and directed backwards, the rest of the thorax, including collare, pleurae, a narrow square in front of the scutellum, scutellum, metanotum etc. are of a uniform, opaque yellowish-orange. Four first abdominal segments yellowish-orange, with brown incisures; the four following segments black, shining, with a slight metallic, bluish lustre; three velvet-black, opaque, crossbands are placed, the first, at the beginning of the black color, the two others on the incisures. Ovipositor reddish-yellow. Halteres yellow. Legs black, the basis of the femora and the coxae, yellow. Wings of a uniform pale brownish tinge; subcostal cell slightly yellowish; the interval between the auxiliary and the first longitudinal veins a little darker brown; stigma brown.

Hab. Hatam, N. Guinea *(Beccari* July 1874). A single female.

NB. Pachyrrhina tripartita Walk. Proc. Linn. Soc. V, p. 231 (Dorey, N. Guinea), has some points in common with this species, but is too vaguely described for identification. However a « metathorax with an abbreviated black band », is not to be found in *P. melanura.* I could not find that species in the Brit. Mus.

Limnobia spec. One specim. Kandari, Celebes, 1874 *(Beccari).* A true *Limnobia*, of a peculiar type; unfortunately a fragment.

Libnotes simplex n. sp. ♂. Reddish-yellow; antennae brown, except the first joint, which is yellow; wings yellowish hyaline. Length: 9-10 mm.

(The specimen is imperfectly preserved). Rostrum and first joint of antennae yellow; antennae and palpi brown; the latter yellow at the root; joints of the flagellum distinctly pedicelled, the two first short, subglobular, the following subcylindrical, slightly incrassated near the base (with a single long hair on each incrassation), each successive joint increasing in length and

diminishing in breadth; last joint long and slender; front and
vertex brownish-gray, with some blackish pile. Thoracic dorsum
brownish-yellow, opaque, without apparent stripes; pleurae
nearly of the same color, faintly shining and almost imperceptibly
pruinose; scutellum and metathorax yellowish; the latter
with some faint brown shadows; abdomen almost uniformly
brownish-yellow, with a brownish dorsal stripe; genitals purer
yellow. Legs: only a single hind femur is extant, which is
yellow. Wings yellowish-hyaline, veins pale brown, those along
the costa more yellow; the tip of the auxiliary vein is a little
beyond the middle of the inner marginal cell; the crossvein
close by this tip; the end of the first longitudinal vein is incurved
towards the second and connected with the costa by a
crossvein a little distance before its tip; stigma none; the oblique
praefurca is about 1 $1/_4$ the length of the discal cell; great
crossvein opposite the middle of the discal cell; the latter in
the shape of a truncate triangle, the second and third posterior
cells, which form its base, being of the same length; seventh
vein strongly arcuated.

Hab. Ternate, *(Beccari,* 1875). A single male.

Libnotes poeciloptera n. sp. ♂ ♀. Brownish-yellow, thorax with
four brown stripes; wings with numerous brown spots, placed
along the veins. Length: 10-12 mm.

Rostrum and palpi brownish; front reddish. Antennae brownish-yellow;
first joint of scapus brown; joints of the flagellum
of nearly equal length, but gradually diminishing in breadth;
thus, nearer the base they are as broad as long, nearly rounded,
but gradually become more slender and cylindrical; a rudimental
15th joint at tip; besides a microscopic pubescence,
perceptible only under a strong lens, only a few longer hairs
are visible, and they are not longer than the joints themselves.
(The antennae of the ♀ are damaged at the tip). Thoracic dorsum
brownish-yellow, intermediate brown stripes approximate;
lateral ones abbreviated. Scutellum yellow, metathorax brownish.
Abdomen, including the genitals, reddish-yellow. Halteres yellow

(with brown knob in the specimen from Java). Legs yellow, a
faint brown ring a short distance before the tip of the femora;
extreme tip of tibiae and tarsi infuscated. Wings with a pale-
yellowish tinge and with numerous brown clouds along the
veins; these clouds are long and narrow and present the appearance as if the whole vein was clouded, but with longer or
shorter lighter colored interruptions; the clouds on the crossveins
are larger and rounder; some illdefined, interrupted clouds
along the hind margin. Venation: the auxiliary vein reaches to
the middle of the inner marginal cell and the crossvein is
close by its tip; the first longitudinal vein is incurved towards
the costa; the marginal crossvein is rather remote from the
tip of the first longitudinal vein: praefurca oblique and very
short; discal cell long and narrow; the second posterior cell
longer than the third, as its base nearly reaches the middle of
the discal cell.

Hab. Mt. Singalang, Sumatra *(Beccari,* July 1878). A single
male. A female from Java *(Müller)* in the Leiden Museum.

Teucholabis bico'or n. sp. ♂. Black, shining, collare yellow,
tip of wings and a crossband in the middle, blackish. Length:
5-6 mm.

Head black, upper part of rostrum brownish-yellow; antennae
black, yellowish at base; collare and fore coxae bright yellow.
Thorax black, shining; abdomen, including the genitals, black.
Stem of halteres blackish, knob yellow. Legs: femora yellow,
except the tip, which is black, tibiae yellowish brown, with a
black tip; tarsi blackish brown. Wings with a yellowish tinge;
the tip blackish, this color occupying a little more than half
the distance between the tip and the central crossveins; a rather narrow blackish crossband runs between the costa and the
hind margin, where it covers the tip of the seventh vein.

Hab. Mount Singalang, Sumatra, July 1878 *(Beccari);* a single
male. — Another specimen (♂), also from Sumatra *(Müller)*
in the Museum in Leiden; it has the whole head brownish-
yellow.

NB. The genus *Teucholabis* is abundantly represented in North and South-America, but hitherto has not been known to occur anywhere else. *T. bicolor* reproduces exactly the characteristics of the genus, the somewhat prolonged rostrum, the hairy legs, the peculiar venation; even the structure of the forceps, as far as I can ascertain, seems to be the same as that of the N. American *T. complexa,* which I have described in the Monogr. N. Am. Dipt. IV, p. 129, Tab. III, f. 9.

Gynoplistia jucunda n. sp. ♂ ♀. Four posterior cells; thorax black, shining, abdomen reddish-yellow; wings tinged with yellow, and with several blackish marks. Length ♂: 10-11 mm.

Head black and shining above; reddish-yellow are the face, the palpi, the mouthparts and the underside of the head; antennae reddish-yellow at base, darker towards the end. Collare yellow; thorax black, shining above. Legs reddish-yellow; tibiae (especially in the ♀) more brownish; tarsi still darker, except at the base. Abdomen, including halteres reddish-yellow. Wings tinged with yellowish, which color is more saturate in the costal cell; apex faintly tinged with blackish; a brown cloud at the origin of the praefurca; stigma, and cloud extending from it along the central crossveins, brown; great crossvein and that, closing the discal cell, also with a very narrow and faint brownish border; a faint cloud in the middle of the sixth vein; seventh vein undulating.

Hab. Kandari, in Celebes; April 1874 *(Beccari).* A single ♂. I saw a male and a female from Sula in the Brit. Mus. under the above name.

NB. In this species, the *six* first joint of the flagellum have each a single branch; the branches are all of the same length, except the first, which is a little shorter; all are on the inner side of the antenna; the two first, are directed downwards, the others horizontally inwards (supposing the antenna to be extend horizontally forwards); the following joints (beginning with the seventh of the flagellum) are without branches, (their number cannot be stated, as the tips are broken off). The branches in the female are but a little shorter. The brown marks on the wings of the ♀ are more intense, the cloud on the 6ᵗʰ vein is connected by a brown stripe with a spot at the proximal end of the basal cells; there is a cloud on the seventh vein.

G. jucunda differs from the typical species of the genus in having a lesser number of branches to the antennae and only *four* posterior cells; the proximal ends of the 2ᵈ and 3ᵈ posterior cells are equidistant from the root of the wing. The same is the case with the first posterior and the first submarginal cells; the second submarginal has its proximal end a little nearer to the root of the wing.

The forceps of the ♂ seems to resemble the normal forceps of the *Limnophilina*.

Eriocera morosa n. sp. ♀. Altogether black, including legs and halteres; wings brown. Length: 13-14 mm. (without the ovip.).

Head with a brownish-gray pollen, on a black ground, especially along the eyes, and with, black, erect hairs on the front; flagellum of the antennae brownish-black, hairy. Thoracic dorsum black, opaque, hairy; some ill-defined spots of brownish-gray pollen along its anterior margin which become more distinct in an oblique light; pleurae brownish-black, somewhat shining. Abdomen velvet-black, opaque, but the anterior portion of every segment less intensely black, and somewhat shining; ovipositor long and slender, brownish-ferruginous. Wings uniformly brown, with a slight violaceous reflection; a short stump of a vein near the origin of the praefurca; discal cell but very little longer than broad, nearly square; bases of the second and third posterior cells nearly in a line; great crossvein opposite the middle of the discal cell. Legs brownish black, with a dense, but short pubescence.

Hab. Kandari, Celebes (*Beccari,* April 1874). — A single female.

Eriocera selene n. sp. ♀. Thorax, including coxae, red; abdomen black; wings brown, with a crescent-shaped white spot and white tip. Length 12-13 mm.

Head black, with a gray pollen and black pile ; scapus of antennae black, flagellum brownish-yellow. Thorax of a rather uniform, saturate, dark orange-red, opaque. Halteres and legs brown. Abdomen black, moderately shining, incisures opaque; last segment and ovipositor reddish. Wings of a uniform brown (of moderate intensity); an oblong, almost crescent-shaped white spot in the middle, between the first and the fifth vein (the latter it does not touch) and immediately before the bifurcation of the second vein; the extreme tip of the wing also white. The crossvein at the base of the 3^a post. c. is placed obliquely; the great crossvein is in a line with it. The tip of the auxiliary vein is opposite the marginal crossvein ; the latter being some distance beyond the proximal end of the submarginal cell.

Hab. Mt. Singalang, Sumatra, July 1878 *(Beccari)*. One female.

RHYPHIDAE.

Rhyphus sp. One specim., Sorong, N. Guinea, May 1872 *(D'Albertis)*.

This is the first *Rhyphus* recorded from the Archipelago; species have been described however from New Zealand and Tasmania. The specimen (in very bad condition) does not seem to have anything to distinguish it from the ordinary type of the genus.

XYLOPHAGIDAE.

Subula inamoena Walk. (*Solva*), J. Pr. Lin. Soc. IV, 98 ! (Celebes).

Two ♀, Kandari, Celebes, April 1874 *(Beccari)*.

The type has the abdomen black above with yellow incisures; tip of the antennae also black ; nevertheless it is very probably the same species.

NB. There is no necessity for a new genus *Solva* Wk.; it is simply a *Subula*, closely resembling in structure and coloring

the european and north-american species. The fourth posterior
and the anal cells are closed at a greater distance from the
margin of the wing than in the european *S. marginata;* and the
tip of the fourth p. c. is *not* connected by a vein with the
margin ; the second vein, issuing from the discal cell is interrupted before reaching the margin , the same as in *S. marginata.* I have not noticed in the Brit. Mus. the *Solva hybotoides*
Wk. l. c. VI, 5. (Gilolo).

Subula *flavipes* Dol., 3ᵈᵉ Bijdr. 13, I would have taken for the
same as *S. inamoena ,* if the antennae 'were not said to be
brown.

Rhachicerus zonatus n. sp. ♀. Antennae and legs rufous, abdomen black, with an obscure reddish crossband at the base of
the second segment. Long. corp. 12-13 mm. (without the ovipositor).

Palpi and antennae rufous, as well as the part of the front
immediately above the root of the antennae ; antennae with
30-31 joints; the joints of the flagellum , except the last, are
provided on the underside with branches, forming a dense comb;
front and vertex black, shining ; occiput dark reddish. Thoracic
dorsum brownish-yellow ; humeral callosities paler yellow ; behind
each, an interrupted black stripe, not reaching the root of the
wing ; two ill-defined black, parallel stripes, almost coalescent
on their inner side , occupy the middle of the dorsum and
nearly reach the scutellum ; the latter yellowish-red. Pleurae :
the portion between root of wings and front coxae black, shining ; the rest reddish-brown; metathorax yellowish-brown ,
brownish in the middle. Halteres: stem yellowish-brown ; knob
brown. Abdomen black, shining ; at the base of the second segment a dark, reddish crossband. Legs rufous, including coxae ;
root of hind coxae brown ; extreme tip of hind tibiae and two
or three last joints of tarsi, brownish. Wings subhyaline, with a
brownish cloud between the costa and the proximal end of the
discal cell ; the latter half of the wings , beyond the central
crossveins is slightly tinged with grayish.

Hab. Mount-Singalang, Sumatra; July 1878 *(Beccari)*.

NB. I. *Antidoxion fulvicorne* Snellen v. Vollenh., Versl. en Medd. K. Akad. Wetensch. 1863, f. 1-3 (Q) from Java, is very like *R. zonatus,* but differs in being a little larger; the antennae are comparatively longer, the thorax and abdomen have more red in their coloring; the wings have a more brownish tinge, especially on the distal half; the cloud in the middle is much larger; the halteres altogether reddish. It is singular that Snellen v. Vollenhoven attributes 26 joints to the antennae; his own type in Leiden (which I saw) has 34-35 joints. The number of joints may be differently counted, as the first and last joints of the flagellum show a slight suture.

NB. II. There is no reason to separate *Antidoxion* from *Rhachicerus.* I have compared *R. zonatus* with an american species, and have not found anything to justify the separation. A species from Brazil, in the Vienna Museum (Q, Coll. Beschke, in the Winthem Collect.) is not unlike *R. zonatus,* especially in the structure of the antennae; but I counted only 22 joints on them. Thus we have now this genus from North-America and Cuba (5 spec.), South-America (one sp.), the East Indian Archipelago (2 sp.) and Spain (one species, described by Loew, in Beschr. Eur. Dipt. I, 248).

STRATIOMYIDAE.

Campeprosopa munda n. sp. σ. Thorax metallic bluish-green; abdomen metallic-blue, 2^d and 3^d segments brownish-yellow, with a square, metallic-blue spot on each side; apex of the wings infuscated. Long. corp. 8-9 mm.

Head black, front narrow, almost linear; antennae black; proboscis pale yellow. Thorax metallic bluish green, but little shining, as it is microscopically punctate and clothed with an appressed, not very dense, yellowish pubescence; a longer and more whitish pubescence on the pleurae; a smooth, shining, metallic blue or green space between the root of the wings and the collare. Scutellum like the thorax in color, sculpture and pubescence; its extreme end, as well as the two long spines upon it, are yellow or reddish. Abdomen: first segment metallic blackish-blue; the second and third are reddish-yellow; each of them has, on each side, a square, metallic purplish blue spot, which does not touch any of the margins of the segment; the interval between the right and left spot of each segment is as broad, or a little broader than the spots themselves; segments 4 and 5 are metallic purplish-blue; genitals pale-yellow. Halteres yellow; coxae pale-yellow; the last pair are dark at base; femora reddish-yellow, the last pair slightly infuscated at base and on the upper side at tip; front tibiae yellow, sometimes brownish towards the end; middle tibiae brownish, paler about the middle; hind tibiae black; tarsi brown, the first joint of the two anterior pairs pale yellow, infuscated at tip. Wings nearly hyaline; apex infuscated, the infuscation not reaching the discal cell, but extending as a gray shadow along the posterior margin; stigma black; a brownish cloud in the first basal cell, below the stigma.

Hab. Mount Singalang, Sumatra, July 1878; two specimens.

NB. There is no doubt that this species belongs in the genus *Campeprosopa* Macq. Suppl. 4, 46; it even bears a certain likeness to *C. flavipes* Macq., as represented l. c. Tab. 5, f. 4. In the Museum in Leiden I saw several specimens determined *C. flavipes* Macq., which were much more like mine, than that figure; they differed in having the end of the hind femora more decidedly black, the hind tibiae with a yellow crossband in the middle and the hind tarsi white, except at the base, which was black; the dark color of the apex of the wing was somewhat evanescent.

Ephippium festinans Wk. (*Clitellaria*) J. Proc. Lin. Soc. IV, 95! (Celebes).

Three ♂, one ♀; Kandari, Celebes, April 1874 *(Beccari)*.

Ephippium maculipenne Macq. (*Clitellaria*) D. E. Suppl. IV, 54, 3 (Manilla).

Four ♀, one ♂. Ramoi and Dorei Hum, N. Guinea, Febr. 1875; Ternate 1875 *(Beccari)*.

Agrees well; compare also the additions by Schiner, Novara, 53. In the Vienna Museum there are specimens from Cape York (Thorey). — *Odontomyia cinerea* Dol. 2de Bijdr. 27 (Amboina) is perhaps the same species; the description of the legs disagrees; the abdomen cannot be called steel-blue. This species and the former would have to be placed, I suppose, in the genus *Nigritomyia* Bigot.

Odontomyia sp. One ♂; Java *(Beccari* 1875).

Odontomyia sp. One ♀; Java *(Beccari* 1875).

(?) **Odontomyia immiscens** Wk. *(Stratiomys)* J. Pr. Lin. Soc. IV, 94 (Celebes).

One ♀; Kandari, Celebes, April 1874 *(Beccari)*.

Walker describes a male and hence, the description does not agree well; but I saw the type in the Br. Mus. and believe, that my female specimen may be the same species.

Hermetia cerioides Walk. *(Massicyta)* J. Proc. Lin. Soc. III, 79! (Aru, Gilolo, Batchian).

Two ♂; Sorong, N. Guinea *(L. M. D'Albertis,* May 1872); Ternate 1875 *(Beccari)*.

Fresh specimens seem to have green, instead of yellow, spots on the body; hence the mention of green in Mr. Walker's description, which is unrecognisable. — Wheter this species is congeneric with *Massicyta bicolor* Wk., the type of the genus, I cannot decide, not having examined the latter. *H. cerioides* has very little to distinguish it from a regular *Hermetia*.

Acanthina obesa Wk. *(Citellaria)* J. Proc. Lin. Soc. V, 233! (Dorei, New Guinea; in the *Synopsis* also from the Philippines, Batchian and Ceram).

Four ♂, Ramoi and Andai, N. Guinea (febr. 1875, Beccari; June, Aug. 1872, *L. M. D'Albertis)*.

Is very like *A. azurea* Gerst. from Ceylon (the only species of the old continent hitherto described), but seems to differ in the coloring of the vertex and in the position of the silvery stripes of the thorax (if I understand Mr. Gerstaecker's description).

(?) **Salduba gradiens** Wk. J. Pr. Lin. Soc. VII, 203! (Mysol). One ♂; Ramoi, N. Guinea, Febr. 1875 *(Beccari)*.

Salduba singularis, areolaris, venosa, as well as *gradiens* look very much alike; but the description of the last one comes nearest to the specimen before me. The type in the Br. M. however, has no yellow at the root of the wings, and hence the identification is not quite certain.

(?) **Salduba singularis** Wk. J. Proc. Lin. Soc. V, 272 (Batchian). One ♂; Ramoi, N. Guinea, Febr. 1875 *(Beccari)*.

Seems to differ from the former in the color of the legs (less white at the root of hind tarsi), the much more distinct spines on the hind femora etc. Nevertheless the specimen is too imperfectly preserved to admit of any certainty.

Ptilocera smaragdina Snellen v. Vollenh. Mem. Entomol. etc. I, 92, 1857.

I have about 30 specimens before me, most of them from Celebes, three from Ternate, three from N. Guinea and one from Amboina. I am unable to make out that *P. amethystina* S. v. V. is a different species. The specimens that look most smaragdine from one point of view, will look amethystine from another. In two of the specimens (both females, one from Amboina, the other from N. Guinea) the greater part of the anal cell and a portion of the fourth posterior are almost hyaline, while the interval between the anal cell and the costal margin is much darker brown than the distal half of the wing. The amethystine reflection of these specimens is a little mere permanent; their size is a little larger than the average of the other specimens. They may belong to *amethystina* v. Voll., although I am by no means satisfied about their specific distinctness.

Tinda modifera Walk. J. Pr. Lin. Soc. IV, 101! (Celebes).

SYN. **Phyllophora bispinosa** Thomson, Eug. R. 454,16 (Manilla).

Four ♂, Kandari, Celebes, April 1874 *(Beccari)*.

Agrees well, but the scutellum (even in the typical specimen) has only four spines, and not *six*, as Walker has it.

Phyllophora angusta Wk. l. c. 7 (Singapore) I would take for *Tinda* if it was not for the mention of « two cinereous stripes on the thorax ».

NB. That *Tinda* is the same as *Phyllophora* Macq. D. E. I, 1, 178, Tab. 22, f. 1 (an african species), is far from certain, the data in Macquart's description being insufficient. The elongated terminal portion of the third antennal joint in *T. modifera* is more than three times as long as the coalescent three portions forming the base of that joint; in *Phylloph. nigra* it is said to be only twice as long, and has a different shape (lanceolate and not linear). The front in Macquart's figure (1 and 1 *a*) is represented as much larger than that of *Tinda modifera*. The name *Phyllophora* is, at any rate preoccupied.

The identity of *Tinda* with *Elasma* Jaenn. Neue Exot. Dipt. 14, Tab. I, f. 3, I look upon as almost certain ; the peculiarities of the venation (absence of the small crossvein, the third vein apparently issuing from the side of the discal cell) common to both, are especially convincing. The last antennal joint is figured by Jaennicke as narrower than that of *Tinda*. The species, *E. acanthinoidea* (Java) must be different from *T. modifera,* the thorax being more coarsely punctate, the pleurae and abdomen whitish pubescent, etc.

Rosapha habilis Walk. J. Pr. Lin. Soc. IV, 100! (Celebes, also the Philippines in the Synopsis).

SYN. **Calochaetis bicolor** Bigot, Ann. S. Ent. Fr. 1879, 189 (Manilla).

One ♀, Kandari, Celebes, April 1874 *(Beccari)*.

Description recognizable ; but the scutellum has four spines, and not two ; the color of the abdomen varies in the extent of the black; the black spot in front of the thorax is sometimes wanting.

I have specimens from the Philippines (Prof. C. Semper), which differ in having the brown stigma separated from the subapical brown cloud, by a broad hyaline interval; the intermediate pair of spines on the scutellum is comparatively smaller; but I do not perceive any other differences. Mr Bigot's description applies to these specimens. Mr Walker recognized his *R. habilis* in them; they may nevertheless be a different species.

NB. Rosapha is easily distinguished from *Tinda:*

The antennae are comparatively longer; the elongated last joint has a distinct, although very short, fringe of microscopic hairs on both sides (as in *Hermetia*); in *Tinda* a similar, but much less distinct fringe is perceptible on one side only.

The thorax is a little more narrowed anteriorly; in *Tinda*, its sides are nearly parallel.

The four scutellar spines are much longer and stouter here and the intermediate pair is much larger than the lateral ones. In the specimen from Celebes the intermediate pair, in consequence of its size, overshadows entirely the much smaller lateral pair; it is not quite so large, however, in the specimens from the Philippines. In *Tinda*, the four spines are short, of about egual length and the hind margin of the scutellum is marked off by a distinct groove.

The anterior crossvein is quite distinct, and hence, the proximal end of the first basal cell square; in *Tinda* it forms a point, in consequence of the absence of the small crossvein; in other respects the venation shows but little difference.

The ♂ has the eyes contiguous for a considerable space above the antennae; in the ♀ they are separated by a moderately broad front (broader above than below).

Nerua impendens Wk. J. Pr. Lin. Soc. IV, 97! (Celebes).
Nine ♂, one ♀; Kandari, Celebes, April 1874 *(Beccari)*.
The description agrees quite well.

N. scenopinoides Wk. J. Proc. Lin. Soc. III, 81 ! (Aru, Waigiou, Batchian).

SYN. **Evasa pallipes** Bigot, Ann. Soc. Entom. 1879, 220 (Batchian).

One ♂, two ♀. Dorei Hum, N. Guin. Febr. 1875 *(Beccari);* Andai, N. Guin. 1872 *(L. M. D'Albertis).*

The female has more yellow at the end of the scutellum, than the male; the knob of the halteres is brown. The description agrees tolerably well.

Nerua mollis n. sp. ♂♀. Abdomen brownish-yellow; wings hyaline; marginal and submarginal cells dark brown. Length: 5-6 mm.

Stouter than *N. impendens* and *scenopinoides,* the wings comparatively longer and broader. Antennae yellowish, arista brown; head black; front, above the antennae, densely grayish-pollinose. Thorax black, shining, clothed with a dense, short yellowish pubescence. Edge of the scutellum and its spines, yellow. Halteres yellow, hardly tinged with brownish at the base of the knob. Abdomen brownish-yellow; in the ♀ more brownish towards the end and on the sides. Legs yellow, front tarsi brown; tips of the other tarsi also more or less brown; in the ♂ the front femora and tibiae are somewhat infuscated in the middle. Wings hyaline, veins pale brownish; the stigma, the marginal and submarginal cells dark brown, which color encroaches upon the first posterior cell at its distal end only, in the shape of a pale cloud.

Hab. Mt. Singalang, Sumatra, July 1878 *(Beccari).* Two specimens.

NB. Evasa fulviventris Bigot, Ann. S. E. Fr. 1879, 220 (Moluccae) also has a yellowish abdomen; but the dense pubescence of the thorax is not mentioned, nor do other parts of the description apply to my specimens. *E. bipars* Wk. has the wings colored differently.

The well defined brown border of the wings, not overstepping the third vein, except at its end, and in marked contrast

to the clearness of the rest of the wing, easily distinguishes
N. mollis from the two preceding species.

Sargus repensans Wk. J. Pr. Lin. Soc. IV, 96 (Celebes)!
Nine ♂, one ♀; Kandari, Celebes, April 1874 *(Beccari)*.
Walker should not have called the wings *cinereous;* otherwise
the description is recognizable.

Sargus remeans Wk. J. Pr. Lin. Soc. IV, 96 (Celebes)!
One ♂; Kandari, Celebes, Apr. 1874 *(Beccari)*.
Fifteen other specimens (among them only one ♀), from the
same locality are smaller, the abdomen narrower, wings a little paler brown; on the second segment there are two large
yellowish-white spots, contiguous near the base of the segment,
separated beyond it by a narrow brown stripe. These spots
also exist in the other, larger specimen, but they are small,
almost rudimentary. In other respects these specimens resemble
Sargus remeans. I label them *remeans,* with *a doubt.*

Sargus rogans Wk. J. Pr. Lin. Soc. III, 81 (Aru Isl[ds])!
One ♂; Dorei Hum, N. Guinea, Febr. 1875 *(Beccari)*.
The description agrees well; the type in the Br. Mus. is damaged and hardly recognizable. *S. ferrugineus* Dol. is closely
allied, but has no brown spots on the abdomen; neither is the
brown cloud near the apex of the wings mentioned in the description. *Plecticus Doleschalli* Bigot, Ann. S. Ent. Fr. 1879, 231
(Mysol) is probably the same species as *S. rogans.*

Sargus quadrifasciatus Wk. J. Pr. Lin. Soc. V, 274 (Bat-
chian)!
One ♂; Dorei Hum, N. Guinea, Febr. 1875 *(Beccari)*.
The color of the abdomen seems to vary as to the extent of
the black; hence I believe that a ♀ from Ternate likewise be-
longs here. *S. rufescens* v. d. Wulp, Tijdschr., etc. 1868, 104,
Tab. III, f. 7-9, is a species of the same group.
NB. Sargus rogans and *quadrifasciatus,* perhaps also *repensans*

belong in the genus *Plecticus* Loew. *S. remeans* also has some
of the characters of that genus (structure of 2^d antennal joint
etc.), but the structure of the ♂ genitals is different, as well
as the general coloring, which is brown, while yellow is the
prevailing color among the species of *Plecticus.*

Sargus mactans Wk. J. Pr. Lin. Soc. IV, 97 (Celebes).
Three specim.; Kandari, Celebes, Apr. 1874 *(Beccari);* one
from Ternate (id.). There may be several conflicting species
here, or else they vary in the extent of the black on the legs
and in the color of the stigma. *S. mactans* has yellow legs, but
the hind tibiae black at base. *S. formicaeformis* Dol., 2de Bijdr.
26 (Amboina) may be this species, but the description is too
vague.

Microchrysa annulipes Thoms. Eugen. Resa, 461 (Manilla).
One ♀, Ternate, 1875 *(Beccari).*
The wings of the specimen are soiled, and thus I could not
identify that part of M.ʳ Thomson's description.

Microchrysa flaviventris Wied. (*Sargus*) Auss. Zw. II, 40
(Java).
One ♂; Java, 1874 *(Beccari).*

Microchrysa sp. — Mt. Singalang, Sumatra, July 1878 *(Beccari);* one ♀.

TABANIDAE.

Tabanus succurvus Walk. J. Proc. Lin. Soc. IV, 102! (Makassar, Celebes, Wk.).
Three ♀; Kandari, Celebes, April 1874 *(Beccari).*
M. Walker's description is recognizable.

Tabanus insurgens Wk. J. Pr. Lin. Soc. V, 276! (Batchian, Wk.).

Two ♀; Dørei Hum and Ramoi, N. Guinea, Febr. 1875 *(Beccari)*.

M. Walker describes a ♂, hence the identification is doubtful. The type, which I saw, seems to be the same species as mine.

Tabanus papuinus Wk. J. Pr. Lin. Soc. VIII, 108. (N. Guinea Wk.).

One ♀, Sorong, N. Guinea, 1872 *(L. M. D'Albertis)*.

M. Walker describes a male, nevertheless the description agrees tolerably well.

Tabanus. One ♀, Korido, N. Guinea, 1875 *(Beccari)*.

Tabanus. One ♀, Mt. Singalang, Sumatra, July 1878 *(Beccari)*.

Tabanus. One ♀, Kaju Tanam, Sumatra, Aug., Sept. 1878 *(Beccari)*.

Chrysops albicinctus v. d. Wulp. Tijdschr. v. Ent. XI, 1868, p. 103, Tab. 3, f. 6. *(Salwatti)*.

Three ♀, Hatam, N. Guinea, June 1875; Salwatti, N. Guin. Decemb. 1875 *(Beccari)*.

Wiedemann's description of *C. pellucidus* Fab. (Tranquebar), short as it is, is quite well applicable to this species; but I adopt the other name, as more certain.

Differs from the ordinary type of *Chrysops* in the broad, flattened third antennal joint and stouter tibiae.

Chrysops dispar (Fab.) Wied. Auss. Zw. I, 196 (East-Indies).

Seven ♀ from Buitenzorg, Java, 1875 *(Ferrari)*.

The identification is certain, altho' there are discrepancies, especially in the description of the face; — Macquart, D. E. I, 1, 159 notices the same differences.

Silvius (?) dimidiatus v. d. Wulp, Tijdschr. v. Ent. XI, 1868, 102, Tab. 3, f. 3-5 (!).

One ♀, Dorei Hum, New Guinea, Febr. 1875 *(Beccari)*. I have no doubt that this is but a less dark variety of the same species. The femora, and in part also, the tibiae, instead of black, are yellowish rufous; the abdomen is only slightly infuscated on the posterior margin of segments 2-5. The wings agree exactly; (there is a slight inaccuracy in the extent of the brown design, as given in the figure; the first submarginal cell should be nearly filled out with brown; the crossband should be less pointed, broader, posteriorly). — It is *not* a true *Silvius*, because the antennae have a different shape and the eyes show a trace of a broad crossband, while the known species of *Silvius* have greenish eyes, dotted with black.

Haematopota irrorata Macq. D. E. I, 1, 163; Tab. XIX, f. 3. (Java).

Four ♀. Mt. Singalang, Sumatra, July 1878 *(Beccari)*. I determine this species in agreement with M.ʳ V. d. Wulp, who showed me three, closely allied species from Sumatra, but which could easily be distinguished by the arrangement of the spots at the tip of the wing. Macquart's description shows slight discrepancies.

H. pungens Dol. (Java) may be the same species, but the description is too incomplete.

LEPTIDAE.

Chrysopila ferruginosa Wied. *(Leptis)* Auss. Zw. I, 224 (Java). Eighteen ♂♀; Ternate 1875 *(Beccari)*.

Four ♂; Kandari, Celebes, April 1874 *(id.)*.

Two ♂, one ♀ from Dorei Hum, N. Guinea 1875 *(id.)*.

The males from Ternate and New Guinea have brown incisures on the abdominal segments, which the females have not. The males from Celebes do not have these incisures. Are they the same species? Wiedemann describes a male, but does not mention those incisures. Some specimens, especially those from New Guinea have the distal half of the wings much more infuscated.

C. insularis Schin. Novara, 199 is a closely resembling species. *Heliomyia ferruginea* Dol., 2de Bijdr. 26, is probably the same as *ferruginea,* although some points of the description do not agree.

Chrysopila vacillans Wk. J. Proc. Linn. Soc. III, 89! (Aru Isl.^{ds}).

One ♀; Aru Islands, Wokan, 1873 *(Beccari).*

The description is bad, nevertheless the identification probable. The type in the Br. Mus. is in poor condition, but seems to be the same species.

Two ♂ (Dorei Hum, N. Guinea, Febr. 1875, *Beccari*) are larger; the occiput is silvery white (*Chr. vacillans* has on the occiput two silvery-white spots, on velvet-black ground, immediately behind the vertex; the lower portion of the occiput alone is white, which color extends upwards along the posterior orbit of the eye); the abdomen in reddish, except a brown crossband on the second segment and a brown tip; the second posterior cell is expanded (encroaching upon the first) and in the expansion there is an oblong hyaline spot, which is beautifully opalescent, as well as the other hyaline parts of the wing. It is not impossible that this is simply the other sex of *vacillans;* in the Br. Mus. I did not find any specimen which resembled these males.

The shortness of the 3^d posterior cell, in comparison to the second and the opalescence of the hyaline portions of the wing, are the most striking characters of the above mentioned ♂ and ♀ specimens, whether they belong to the same species or not. Walker describes two other species *C. guttipennnis* and *stylata,* of the same group. If they are really different, it will be interesting to ascertain whether the above described expansion of the second posterior cell is a sexual or a specific character? I have not examined these species in detail.

Chrysopila lupina n. sp. ♀. Body yellowish-tawny, head black; wings with an interrupted brown crossband, which is connected with a brown apical margin. Long. corp. 7-8 mm. (without the ovipositor).

Proboscis and palpi tawny; face pale yellowish-gray (somewhat injured in the specimen); front and vertex (♀) black, except a narrow stripe above the antennae, which is silvery; basal joints of the antennae yellowish-tawny, very short; third joint also small, black; the black arista, under a strong lens, appears finely pubescent. Thorax tawny; the dorsum opaque, without any apparent stripes; pleurae a little paler, nearly opaque, except a shining space above the middle coxae. Legs yellowish-tawny, tibiae brownish, tarsi brown. Halteres tawny. Abdomen brownish-tawny, hind margins of segments faintly brownish. Wings with a slight yellowish tinge. A brown crossband issues from the dark brown stigma, runs across the marginal cell and fills out the proximal end of the submarginal, where it does not cross the third vein; a moderately broad apical margin begins immediately beyond the stigma, is broadest at the intersection of the veins and has an indentation within each of the cells which it crosses; becoming narrower posteriorly, it partly fills out third posterior cell, and coalesces with a brown cloud on the distal crossveins of the discal cell. (In other words, the brown crossband of the wings is interrupted by the whole breadth of the first posterior cell and becomes confluent with the apical brown border of the wing by means of the third posterior cell; it does not encroach upon the fourth posterior cell).

Hab. Mt. Singalang (Sumatra), July 1878; *Beccari;* one female.

NB. This species has the appearance and coloring of a *Leptis.* I place it in *Chrysopila* on account of the anal cell being closed some distance from the margin. But the palpi are broad and flattened, almost spatulate; the face is not as concave as in *Chrysopila;* nor does the silky pubescence, which characterizes the latter genus, exist here. But *Leptis ferruginosa* Wied. placed in the genus *Chrysopila* by Schiner, can only artificially find a place in it, and the genus *Heliomyia* established for it by Doleschall, but rejected by Schiner, may be revived yet. The face of *C. lupina* shows the same bladderlike swelling as *C. ferruginosa;* and the female of the latter also has spatulate palpi, which is therefore a sexual caracter.

Leptis uniguttata n. sp. ♂. Abdomen yellow, with black crossbands, black at tip; wings uniformly brown, with a hyaline spot in the second basal cell. Long. corp. 7-8 mm.

Antennae yellowish; frontal triangle (above the antennae) gray; vertical triangle gray in front, black behind (around the ocelli). Thorax grayish-black above, humeral callosities and a spot in front of the scutellum, pale yellowish; pleurae grayish; scutellum black; halteres with a black knob, stem brown. Abdomen: first segment yellow ; segments 2-4 yellow, with a broad black crossband, occupying nearly the whole segment, except a very narrow anterior and a broader posterior margin, which are yellow; the crossband is deep velvet black anteriorly, but less intensely black and more shining, posteriorly; it reaches the lateral margins of the segments, but does not invade the venter, which is yellow; segment five is nearly altogether black, very little yellow being visible on the anterior and posterior margins; segments 5-6 are black on the dorsal, as well as the ventral side; on segm. 5 a little yellow spot is visible on the posterior margin. Legs yellowish-brown; hind femora and tibiae with a broad brown band in the middle; tarsi brownish toward the tip. Wings uniformly colored with brown, except an oblique hyaline spot at the distal end of the second basal cell.

NB. I describe this species, although I have only a single damaged specimen, because it is the only *Leptis* in the collection. The hind femora have, on the underside, near the insertion of the tibiae, a small projection, clothed with short, stiff hairs, which looks like a rudimental femoral spine. I do not find a similar structure in the european species.

Hab. Mt. Singalang, Sumatra, July 1878 *(Beccari).* A single male.

MIDAIDAE.

There are no species of this group in the collection; but I will improve this opportunity in order to insert a notice on *Midas bifascia* Wk. J. Proc. Lin. Soc. IV, 104 (Celebes), which may be useful. Walker says « hind femora and hind tibiae reddish »; and this is really the case with the type (a single specimen) in the British Museum. The museum in Leiden possesses two specimens from Sumatra (Müller) of apparently the same species, but with the hind legs altogether black. I believe therefore that the red hind legs of M. Walker's specimen either represent a variety, or are due to immaturity. The wings may be described as saturate brownish-fulvous (and not « cinereous » as Walker has it), the veins more or less clouded with brown near the apex; that is, very distinctly in one of the specimens, and very little in the other.

ASILIDAE.

Section **Asilina.**

Synolcus xanthopus Wied. Auss. Zw. I, 456 (*Asilus*); compare also v. d. Wulp, l. c. Tab. XI, f. 19.

Two ♂, six ♀. Kandari, Celebes, April 1874 *(Beccari)*.

Mochtherus gnavus v. d. Wulp, Tijdschr. v. Ent. 1872, Tab. XII, f. 3 female; ibid, 1876, 174, male. (Java, Gilolo etc.) 1 ♂, 2 ♀. Kandari, Celebes, April 1874 *(Beccari)*.

Itamus involutus Walk. J. Proc. Lin. Soc. V, 281! (Batchian). One ♀, Ternate, 1875 *(Beccari)*.

M.ʳ Walker describes the ♀; I believe that *I. dentipes* v. d. Wulp, of which I have also seen the type in Leiden, is the male of the same species.

(?) **Itamus longistylus** Wied. Auss. Zw. I, 433 (*Asilus*), Java.
One ♀; Mt. Singalang, Sumatra, July 1878 *(Beccari)*.
The descriptions does not quite agree, both Wiedemann's and
v. d. Wulp's. I have not examined the types in Holland.

Promachus͜complens Walk., J. Proc. Lin. Soc. V, 236! (Dorei, N. Guinea).
One ♀, Momi N. Guinea, 1875 *(Beccari)*.
Although Walker described both sexes, the ♂ alone is preserved in the Br. Mus.; its grayish incisures are broader than
in my specimen. 1 suppose that Walker's words: « which are
most distinct in the male », refer to this difference. In other
respects the agreement is perfect.

Promachus bifasciatus Macq. D. E. I, 2, 98 (*Trupanea*) (Java).

SYN. **Trupanea strenua** Walk. J. Pr. Lin. Soc. IV, 106 (Celebes).

One ♂, Makassar, Celebes, Aug. 1874 *(Beccari)*.

Promachus sp. One ♀; Dorei Hum, N. Guinea, Febr. 1875
(Beccari).
Very like *complens;* but differs especially in the coloring of
the legs.

Promachus sp. Four ♀; Island Yule, N. Guinea, June 1875
(D'Albertis).

Promachus sp. One ♂; Egatpur, Decemb. 1877 *(Beccari)*.

Ommatius fulvidus Wied. Auss. Zw. I, 420 (Java).

SYN. **O. inextricatus** Walk. J. Pr. Lin. Soc. VI, 21! (Ceram).
O. Pennus Walk. List etc. II, 469! (Corea, Borneo).
O. Coryphe Walk. List etc. II, 460! (Patria ?).
O. Androcles Walk. List etc. II, 470! (Sandwich Islands).
Asilus Garnotii Guérin, Voy. de la Coquille, Tab. XX, f. 8 (in the let-
terpress, p. 292, the right name, *fulvidus* W., is given).

Fifteen ♂♀; Amboina, Dec. 1874; Kandari, Celebes, April 1874; Padan Panjan, Sumatra, Aug. 1875 *(Beccari)*. M.ʳ 'V. d. Wulp (Tijdschr. etc. 1872) gives a full description of this species.

Ommatius infirmus v. d. Wulp, Tijdschr. v. Ent. 1872! (Gilolo, Ternate, Morotai).
Six ♂♀; Ternate 1875 *(Beccari)*.

Ommatius spinibarbis v. d. Wulp, Tijdschr. v. Ent. 1872! Gilolo, Borneo, Ternate).
Four ♂♀; Isld. Aru, Wokan, 1873; Ternate *(Beccari)*.

SYN. **Ommatius noctifer** Walk. J. Pr. Lin. Soc. III, 88! (Aru Isld.ᶜ).

Ommatius despectus v. d. Wulp, Tijdschr. etc. 1872! (Java).
Two specim.; Mt. Singalàng, Sumatra, July 1878 *(Beccari)*.

Ommatius sp. Two specim.; Dorei Hum, N. Guinea, Febr. 1875 *(Beccari)*.

Ommatius sp. Six ♂♀; Kandari, Celebes, Apr. 1874 *(Beccari)*.

Ommatius sp. Two ♀; Islds. Aru, Wokan; 1873 *(Beccari)*.

Ommatius sp. One ♀; Dorei, N. Guinea, Decemb. 1875 *(Beccari)*.

The first three species are closely allied; the third resembles *O. infirmus,* except that the two first joints of the antennae are black, instead of yellowish. Although more than 40 species of *Ommatius* from the Malay Archipelago, have already been described (sixteen by Walker from M.ʳ Wallace's collection alone, fifteen new species by M.ʳ v. d. Wulp, besides those, published by Doleschall, Rondani and Schiner) this does not seem to have exhausted the fauna. Still, the further study of this group cannot be pursued now without a very considerable collection.

Section **Leptogastrina.**

Although there are seventeen species of *Leptogaster* from the
Malay Archipelago, described by MM. Doleschall, Walker and
van der Wulp, the two species which I describe below, do not
seem to be among them.

Leptogaster angelus n. sp. ♂. Black, thorax shining, pleurae
hoary; wings crystalline, fork of the third vein not longer than
its petiole. Length: 11-12 mm.

Face whitish, occiput grayish; scapus of the antennae black,
(the rest broken). Thorax black, very bright and shining, with
a slight greenish-metallic lustre; pleurae, pectus, and coxae
silvery-sericeous; posterior portion of the thoracic dorsum grayish pollinose, as well as the scutellum. Abdomen black, with a
slight bluish lustre, especially visible on the proximal half. Halteres with a brown knob. Legs reddish; front pair with the tip
of the femora brown and the base of the tarsi pale yellow;
(middle pair wanting); last pair with the base of the femora
pale yellow, a brown ring before their tip, and the extreme
tip, brown; the hind tarsi have the tips of all the joints brown.
Wings very transparent and colorless (crystalline), veins black;
fork of the third vein unusually short, not much longer than
its petiole; the cell enclosed in it (second submarginal), is very
much coarctate at the tip; the fourth posterior cell is unusually
short, as the intercalary vein issues from the discal cell far
beyond the posterior crossvein (the distance being about equal
to the length of the intercalary vein).

Hab. Kandari, Celebes, April 1874 *(Beccari).* A single male.

Leptogaster inflatus n. sp. ♀. Brown, wings brownish, the
apex subyaline. Length: 13-14 mm.

Antennae black, third joint nearly three times the length of
the scapus, narrow-lanceolate; arista rather stout, not much
longer than the first joint. Face with a brownish-golden pube-

scence; front brownish-pollinose, vertex black. Thorax reddish-brown above, yellowish sericeous on the sides. Abdomen : the first four segments brownish-red, more or less mixed with red : the remainder black; the black portion of the abdomen expanded in breadth (♀). Halteres yellowish, with a brownish knob. Legs brownish ; four front tarsi paler yellowish. Wings tinged with brownish, except the apex, which is subhyaline ; more or less distinct subhyaline streaks in some of the cells; proximal end of the second submarginal nearly on a level with the proximal end of the second posterior; fourth posterior cell long, its proximal end being very near the posterior transverse vein ; discal cell long and narrow.

Hab. Kandari, Celebes, April 1874 *(Beccari)*. Two females.

Leptogaster sp. One specim., Kandari, Celebes *(Beccari)*.

Leptogaster sp. One specim., Kandari, Celebes *(Beccari)*.

Section **Dasypogonina.**

Dasypogon (sensu latissimo) spec. One ♀, Ansus, N. Guinea, 1875 *(Beccari)*.

Belongs in the group provided with a strong hook at the end of the front tibiae and is closely related to *Dasyp. inopinus* Walk. J. Pr. Lin. Soc. III, 83! (Aru Isl.), although different. The antennae, are, unfortunately, broken.

Section **Laphrina.**

Atomosia conspicua v. d. Wulp, Tijdschr. v. Ent. 1872, Tab. XI, f. 3. (Waigiou).

One specim.; Ramoi, N. Guinea, Febr. 1875 *(Beccari)*.

This is the same species as *Laphria placens,* Walk. J. Pr. Lin. Soc. VIII, 110 (New Guinea); but there is an earlier *L. placens* Wk. l. c. III, 128! In the Brit. Mus. the name is changed to *L. amoena,* which name also occurs in M.[r] Walker's

Synopsis; but I do not find this change stated anywhere, and am glad to be able to leave the priority to M.ʳ v. d. Wulp, who has given a fine figure of this species.

Atomosia sp. One ♀. Ramoi, N. Guinea, Febr. 1875 *(Beccari)*. Undoubtedly new, but, unfortunately, in a very bad state of preservation.

Laphria partita Walk. J. Pr. Lin. Soc. IV, 105! (Celebes). One ♂; Kandari, Celebes, Apr. 1874 *(Beccari)*.

Walker says that three abdominal segments are clothed with golden pile (he calls it ochraceous); but the fourth segment (even in the typical specimen) has also a great deal of such pile, and even the fifth, at the basis.

L. auricincta v. d. W. (Timor) must be very like this species, but is described as having the root of the wings only hyaline, and not the whole proximal half, three segments clothed with golden hair; whitish humeral spots etc.; nevertheless it may be the same species. Should the identity be proved, the name would have the priority, as there is an earlier *L. partita* Walker, l. c. I, 115 (Borneo).

Laphria notabilis Macq. D. E. I, 2, 71 (Patria ignota); v. d. Wulp, l. c. Tab. 10, f. 5 and 6.

Syn. **Laphria ardescens** Walk. J. Pr. Lin. Soc. V, 235! (N. Guinea).
L. flagrantissima Walk. l. c. III, 87! (Aru).

Three specimens; Ramoi, N. Guinea, Febr. 1875 *(Beccari)*. The synonymy was made out by M.ʳ v. d. Wulp from the descriptions; I have verified it in the Br. M.

Laphria puer Dolesch. 3ᵈᵉ Bijdr. 15 (Amboina).
♂ ♀, Dorei Hum, Febr. 1875 *(Beccari)*.

Laphria tristis Dolesch. 2ᵈᵉ Bijdr. 22, Tab. II, f. 1! (Amboina). One ♀; Amboina 1873 *(Beccari)*.

Agrees with description and figure. In Vienna, I saw several types of Doleschall, but only one of them entirely agreed with my specimen, in other words, only one of them was a true type of the species. When Schiner Verh. Z. B. Ges. 1867 p. 381, on the strength of one of these types, says that the wings of *tristis* are altogether black («ganz und gar schwarz»), he overlooks Doleschalls description (« alis ima basi pellucidis »), as well as his figure, where the wing is hyaline nearly as far as the discal cell. So much for trusting types, apart from descriptions.

Laphria Taphius Walk. List etc. II, 380! (Philippine islands, Celebes, Amboina).

Two specimens; Kandari, Celebes, April 1874 *(Beccari)*.

Exceedingly like the preceding species, but differs in the front tibiae being beset with whitish pile, and in the hyaline portion of the wings being less extended. I compared my specimen with that in the Br. Mus. which bears M.ʳ Walker's label.

Laphria obliquistriga Walk. J. Pr. Lin. Soc. V, 264! (Celebes).

One ♂; Kandari, Celebes, April 1874 *(Beccari)*.

Agrees with the description, and I find in my notes, taken in the Br. Mus. that the identity may be considered as certain. M.ʳ v. d. Wulp's *obliquistriga* must be, I suspect, a different species; several points in the description are not applicable, especially the direction of the veins closing the discal and fourth posterior cell, which form one line in my specimen. The relation of this species to *L. scapularis* Wied. remains to be investigated, as his type was a female; while Walker's specimen and mine are males. Wiedemanns description disagrees in several respects.

Laphria sp. One ♀. Ramoi, N. Guinea, Febr. 1875 *(Beccari)*.

Related to *L. obliquistriga;* wings much darker, and of the same bluish-brown coloring up to the root; no silvery spots on the thorax, mystax more dense etc.

Laphria sp. One ♂. Mt. Singalang, Sumatra, July 1878 (*Beccari*).

Maira occulta v. d. Wulp, Tijdschr. v. Ent. 1872, Tab. X, f. 12! (Salwatti, Waigiou, N. Guinea).

Two ♀, Fly River, New Guinea, 1876-77 (*L. M. D'Albertis*), and Mansinam, N. Guin. (Coll. Bruijn, 1875). These specimens agree best with M.ʳ v. d. Wulp's description and figure, although the latter, representing perhaps a male, is a little less broad. But I have two other specimens (♂♀, Ramoi, N. Guinea, *Beccari*, Febr. 1875), the exact counterparts of which I have also seen among M.ʳ v. d. Wulp's types of *M. occulta*, but which, nevertheless show some differences. The humeral silvery spots have the shape of a comma, the pointed end of which nearly reaches a silvery spot on the thoracic suture; but, in accordance with M.ʳ v. d. Wulp's description, the specimen, which I take for typical, has the humeral spot double, that is, cut in two by a more or less distinct dark line; it is continued posteriorly, towards the suture, in the shape of an opaque, brownish stripe, without silvery lustre; (« de schouder-vlekken hebben van achteren een bruinen weerschijn, die zich streepvormig tot aan den dwarsnaad voortzet »). The dark portion of the wings of the two specimens from Ramoi is much darker, the hyaline portion less yellowish, than in the specimens from Fly River and Mansinam. For this reason I am in doubt about the specific identity of these specimens.

Maira elysiaca n. sp. ♂. Ground color greenish-coppery, but almost concealed under a dense, closely appressed rufous pubescence; legs with long rufous hair. Long. corp. 28 mm.

There is very little to be added to the diagnosis. The ground-color of the body including the legs is a greenish-bronze color, with coppery reflections; but this color is very much modified on the thoracic dorsum and the abdomen by a dense, short, closely appressed rufous pubescence. Those parts of the body which, in other species are whitish-hoary (humeri, face, pleurae,

coxae) are yellowish-hoary here ; they, as well as the sides of
the head, those of the abdomen, and the legs, are clothed with
long, soft, erect rufous hair , especially long on the legs (the
specimen being a male); the bristles of the mystax and the
single macrochetae on the sides of the abdominal segments,
are all rufous. The wings have a yellowish tinge ; the distal
two thirds of them are brownish ; this color occupies a considerable portion of the anal and axillary cells, but does not invade the two basal cells.

Hab. Korido, N. Guinea *(Beccari);* a single male.

NB. A single specimen of this species (Bouro, Wallace) exists
in the Br. Mus. under the same name *elysiaca,* which I have,
for this reason, adopted. *Laphria paradisiaca* Wk. l. c. III, 128
is very like this species, but the legs are metallic blue, with
long, whitish hairs, the thick pollen on pleurae and coxae is
also whitish, the head is clothed behind with soft, whitish hair,
the abdomen is, comparatively a little less broad.

Maira gloriosa Walk., J. Proc. Linn. Soc. III, 84 ! (Aru).

SYN. **Maira Kollari** (not Dolesch.) v. d. Wulp, Tijdschr. v. Ent. 1872 !

One ♀; Fly River, N. Guinea (*L. M. D'Albertis,* 1876-77).
M.ʳ v. d. Wulp's specimen , which I saw in Leiden , agrees
with mine ; the pubescence of its face is perhaps a little more
whitish. A type of *Laphria Kollari* Dolesch., which I saw in
Vienna is an altogether different species ; it as no appressed
rufous pubescence on the thorax ; nor is this pubescence mentioned in Doleschall's description. That *Maira Kollari* Dol. is
the same species as *M. spectabilis,* as Schiner contends, I do not
think. I believe that M.ʳ v. d. Wulp is right in uniting *L. socia*
Wk. and *consobrina* Wk. with *M. gloriosa* (his *M. Kollari*). I
preferred the name *gloriosa,* because the specimen in the Br.
Mus. came nearest to mine ; the other two, I did not compare
carefully.

Maira spectabilis Guér. Voy. de la Coquille, Zool. II, 292; Tab. 20, f. 7 (*Laphria splendida* on the plate); New Guinea.

SYN. **Laphria congrua** Walk. J. Pr. Lin. Soc. V, 277 (Batchian) (a couple of other of M.ᵣ Walker's species apparently coincide with this).

One ♂, one ♀; Andai, N. Guinea (Coll. Bruijn). I consider this determination as certain, the more so as it agrees with M.ʳ v. d. Wulps. — There is a specimen from Salwatti and another from Ternate, which are more greenish, but may nevertheless belong here.

Maira spec. One ♀, Ramoi, N. Guinea, Febr. 1875 (*Beccari*).

Maira spec. One ♂, Korido, N. Guinea, 1875 (*Beccari*).

NB. Besides the above named species of *Maira*, there are, in the collection some 36 specimens of different species, which I am unable to unravel, nor to identify with the existing descriptions. They may remain untouched for the present and afford the material for a future worker.

Before closing with this genus I must explain that I have called *Maira* all the metallic green and blue species. This genus is not at all well defined by Schiner and its boundary with *Laphria* is still very vague. More attention should be paid to the macrochetae of the abdomen, but especially those on the femora; they may perhaps afford a good character for a closer definition. Some of the species quoted above as *Laphriae* possess such macrochetae on the hind femora and should be better referred to *Maira*.

BOMBYLIDAE.

Argyramoeba semiscita Wk. J. Pr. Lin. Soc. I, 118 (Borneo). One ♀, Kandari, Celebes, April 1874 (*Beccari*).

Doleschall (3ᵈᵉ Bijdr., 21) observes that this species is probably the same as his *A. argyropyga*.

Argyramoeba tripunctata v. d. Wulp, Tijdschr. v. Ent. 1868, 109, Tab. IV, f. 1 (*Salwatti*).

One ♀, Dorei Hum, N. Guinea, Febr. 1875 (*Beccari*).

Argyramoeba sp.

Two ♂, Amboina 1873, Ternate 1875 (*Beccari*).

Exoprosopa chrysolampis Jaennicke, Neue Exot. Dipt. 36, Tab. I, f. 8 (Java).

One specim., Buitenzorg, Java (*Ferrari*).

Exoprosopa coeruleipennis Dolesch. 2de Bijdr. 24 (Amboina).

One specim.; Amboina, Dec. 1874 (*Beccari*).

Exoprosopa doryca Boisduval, Faune de l'Océanie (*Anthrax*), 665. (Dorei, N. Guin.).

SYN. **Anthrax ventrimacula** Dolesch. 2de Bijdr. 23! (Amboina).
Anthrax Pelops Wk. J. Proc. Lin. Soc. III, 90! (New Guinea, Aru, Ternate).
Exoprosopa leuconoe Jaenn. N. Ex. Dipt. 37 (Moluccas).

Four specimens, Amboina, Dec. 1874 (*Beccari*); Mansinam, N. Guin., Nov. 1871 (*L. M. D'Albertis*); Gilolo (Coll. Bruijn).

Walker's second description (l. c. V, 301) seems to refer to a different species. *Hyperalonia oenomaus* Rond. (Borneo) resembles this species very much, but the brown costal border is much broader and occupies the whole of the basal cells and the proximal part of the discal, axillary, and spurious cells.

Lomatia ? or at any rate a very much battered specimen of that group, from Amboina (*Beccari*).

THEREVIDAE.

Ectinorhynchus sp.

One ♂; Hatam, N. Guinea, June 1875 (*Beccari*).

The coloring is very like that of the other species of this

genus. The palpi are concealed in the oral opening, a character which, according to the descriptions, belongs rather to *Anabarhynchus*.

Thereva lateralis (Esch.) Wied. Auss. Zw. I, 231 (Manilla). One ♀; Ternate, 1875 (*Beccari*).

I saw this species named in the same way in Leiden.

CYRTIDAE.

There is a single specimen in the collection (Kapaor, N. Guinea, April 1872; *L. M. D'Albertis*). It has the venation of *Panops* (comp. Macquart, Dipt. Exot. I, 2, Tab. 14, f. 2, *Mesophysa*, which, as Erichson has shown, is the same as *Panops*), as well as the general coloring of most of the species of that genus, dark metallic green body, with a fulvous pubescence on the anterior part of the thorax, yellow legs, etc. It differs from *P. flavipes* Latr. and *Lamarckianus* Westw. in the absence of the minute supplemental cell at the end of the discal; from *P. Baudini* in the coloring of the body and legs. — The proboscis of the specimen is broken off, as in a *Panops* it ought to reach beyond the pectus.

EMPIDAE.

Hybos bicolor Walker, J. P. Lin. Soc. III, 91 (Aru). Two ♂, Islds. Aru, Wokan, 1873 (*Beccari*). The description agrees quite well.

Hybos deficiens Walker, J. Pr. Lin. Soc. III, 129 (Key Isl.[ds]). One specimen, Hatam, N. Guinea, June 1875 (*Beccari*). The description agrees, but the pale hind tarsi are not mentioned in it.

Hybos sp. One specimen, Hatam, N. Guin., 1875 (*Beccari*).

Hybos sp. One specimen, Fly River, (*L. M. D'Albertis*).

DOLICHOPODIDAE.

Paraclius (?) **praedicans** Walk. (*Dolichopus*) J. Pr. Lin. Soc. IV, 115 (Celebes)!

One ♂, two ♀; Kandari, Celebes, April 1874 (*Beccari*).

M. Walker's statement : « cinereous, not metallic » is based upon the fact that his type-specimen was dirty. The thorax is metallic-green, with silvery pleurae. In agreement with the opinion of my friend Prof. Mik, whom I consulted on the subject, I place this species in the genus *Paraclius* Loew, to which it is undoubtedly more related than to any other. Only the last section of the fourth vein is nearly straight, and by no means as much arcuate as in the N. American species of that genus (hitherto the only ones known ; comp. Loew, Monogr. N. Am. Dipt. II, p. 97-100, Tab. III, f. 7); the angle it forms is much more rounded ; the third antennal joint is not rounded at tip (more like l. c. fig. 8 c.).

Diaphorus sp. One specim.; Dorei Hum, N. Guinea (*Beccari*).

All the other *Dolichopodidae* of the collection belong in the genus *Psilopus*, of which there are about *twenty* species. More than *eighty* species of this genus are described from the Malay Archipelago and Australia. I have identified the following two species :

Psilopus aeneus (Fab.) Macq. D. E. II, 2, 116, Tab. 19, f. 3 (Java).

♂ ♀; Aru Islands, Wokan, 1873 (*Beccari*).

Macquart gave a description of Fabricius's types, therefore the identity is not doubtful. Those specimens were males; the female has a more coppery abdomen and the black crossbands are a little broader.

Psilopus crinicornis Wied. Auss. Zw. II, 222 (Java).

♂, Mt. Singalang, Sumatra, July 1878 (*Beccari*).

Although Wiedemann does not describe the gray cloud on the wings, I have little doubt that it is the same species; I also saw it thus determined in Leiden. *Psil. longicornis* Dol. 3ᵈᵉ Bijdr. 22 (Amboina) may be the same species, if the word *tibiis* is substituted to *tarsis* in the description.

SYRPHIDAE.

Baccha vespiformis Dol. II, 35, Tab. III, f. 1! (Amboina).

Four (♂♀) spec.; Kandari, Celebes, April 1874 (*Beccari*).

I have seen Doleschall's types in Vienna; the ♂ has a broad brown crossband on the fourth segment only, the 3ᵈ segment is unicolorous.

Baccha moluccana Dol. II, 36, Tab. III, f. 2 (Amboina).

Two (♂♀) spec.; Ramoi, N. Guinea, Febr. 1875 (*Beccari*).

The types in Vienna agree with this specimen. I believe that the ♂ and ♀ belong together, although the one has a yellow face the other a green metallic one, with dense yellow pollen, leaving only a dark stripe in the middle. The description refers to specimens of the latter kind.

Baccha n. sp.?

One ♀, Gorontalo, Celebes, 1875 (*Beccari*).

I do not describe this species, because, in the coloring of the wings and of the abdomen (especially of the fourth segment), it is exactly like *Baccha apicalis* Loew, Wien. Entom. Monatschr. II, 106 (1858), from Japan. The difference consists in the coloring of the two first abdominal segments and of the legs. The specimen may be a mere variety.

Chilosia sp.

One ♂; Java (*Beccari* 1875).

Belongs in the group with a hairy face, hairy eyes, and with a scutellum with a row of black bristles; arista plumose; etc. (Compare Loew, Verh. Zool. Bot. Ver. 1857). The coloring and general appearance has nothing abnormal. Only a single *Chilosia* has hitherto been described from Asia and Australia; *Chil. australis* Macq. from Tasmania.

Melanostoma orientalis Wied. Auss. Zw. II, 139 (East-Indies). Two ♂; Mt. Singalang, Sumatra, July 1873.

Wiedemann describes a ♀, and hence some discrepancies from his description. Is this species really different from the common *M. scalaris* F.?

Melanostoma sp.

Two ♂, one ♀; Java, Summit of the Pangerango (*Beccari* 1874).

Altogether greenish black, with black legs and antennae: three pairs of reddish spots on the abdomen, on segments 2-4; in one of the ♂ specimens these spots are much smaller than in the other, and the first pair almost evanescent; in the ♀ they are also very small.

Melanostoma sp.

One ♂; Hatam, N. Guinea, June 1875 (*Beccari*). European type. Abdomen red with infuscated incisures; legs red; wings slightly brownish.

Melanostoma sp.

One ♀; Hatam, N. Guinea, June 1875 (*Beccari*). European type; bluish-metallic with white pollen on face and pleurae; abdomen black, opaque, with transverse, shining bands, with a bluish-metallic reflection; legs brownish; wings hyaline.

Syrphus aegrotus (Fab.) Wied. Auss. Zw. II, 118! (Java). Two ♂, Ternate, 1875 (*Beccari*); ♀ Mt. Singalang, Sumatra, July 1878 (id.).

SYN. **Didea Ellenziederi** Dolesch. 2 Bijdr. 31, Tab. X, f. 2 (Amboina).
Syrphus fascipennis Macq. H. N. Dipt. I, 537 [Macq.].
Syrphus infirmus Rond. Ann. Mus. Civico, VII, 423 (Borneo)!

The antennae vary in darkness and are sometimes nearly black; the hyaline space near the root of the wings is sometimes nearly obsolete. In the female from Sumatra the two yellow spots on the second abdominal segment are coalescent and form a continuous crossband; this would answer the *S. infirmus* Rond., the type of which is also a female; the yellow spot on each side of the last abdominal segment, mentioned in the desscription of the latter, is also present in my specimen.

Syrphus salviae (Fab.) Wied. Auss. Zw. II, 122 (Java).

? SYN. **Didea Macquarti** Dolesch. 2 Bijdr. 32, Tab. X, f. 1 (Amboina)!

One ♂, one ♀, Ternate 1875; one ♀ Kandari, Celebes, Apr. 1874; one ♀ Hatam, N. Guinea, June 1875 (*Beccari*).

Wiedemann describes the face as yellowish, the hind tibiae as yellow; Doleschall the face as black, the hind tibiae likewise. I have both forms among my specimens, which in other respects, do not show any difference, but these specimens are not numerous enough to enable me to decide whether these characters are sexual; I therefore assume the synonymy with a doubt.

Syrphus nectarinus Wied. Auss. Zw. II, 128 (China).

SYN. **S. alternans** Macq. D. E. II, 2, 89 (East-Indies) and Suppl. IV, 149 (Australia).
(?) **S. triligatus** Walk. J. Pr. Lin. Soc. I, 19 (Mt. Ophir).

Two spec. ♂♀; Ternate 1875; Java 1874 (*Beccari*).

(?) Syrphus confrater Wied. Auss. Zw. II, 121 (China).

One ♂, one ♀; Mt. Singalang, Sumatra, July 1878; one ♀, Hatam, N. Guinea, June 1875 (*Beccari*).

Type of *S. ribesii, S. americanus* etc. The description agrees, except that the thorax is said to be metallic-blue, instead of greenish. However the species of this group require a much closer description than that of Wiedemann.

Volucella trifasciata Wied. Auss. Zw. II, 196 (Java).
One ♀; Buitenzorg, Java (*Ferrari*).
Agrees well with the description.

Graptomyza gibbula Walk. (*Barytocera*), J. Pr. Lin. Soc. IV, 120 (Celebes).
Three spec.; Kandari, Celebes, April 1874 (*Beccari*).
Is very like *Gr. brevirostris* Wied., but differs in the color of the femora; *Gr. meliponaeformis* Dol. (Amboina) has a yellow scutellum, with a black margin.

Graptomyza spec.
One ♀, Java 1874 (*Beccari*).
Resembles *G. ventralis* Wied. Auss. Zw. II, 207 (Java) very much, only the black coloring on the 3ᵈ and 4ᵗʰ abdominal segments is more extended, and the femora, except the extreme end, are black. In Leiden, where I saw Wiedemann's type, there were two or three closely allied forms, and it may be that they are all varieties of *ventralis*.

Graptomyza lineata n. sp.
One ♀, Ternate 1875 (*Beccari*).
Of the same type with *Graptom. longirostris* Wied., the stature being elongated, the 3ᵈ antennal joint long and narrow, the body marked with longitudinal lines: only the proboscis is not exerted, as in Wiedemann's figure.

Body and legs altogether pale yellow; rostrum with a little brownish above; antennae reddish, upper edge of the third joint brown; arista yellow, brownish towards the tip. Thorax: a longitudinal brown line, placed, one on each side, immediately inside of the humeral callus; they become evanescent before reaching the scutellum; abdomen with three well-marked brown longitudinal stripes, reaching to the tip; halteres and legs yellow, tips of tarsi brownish. Wings hyaline (very much damaged and soiled).

Although the specimen is damaged, perhaps even immature,

I venture to describe it because it will be easily recognizable and represents a peculiar type, very different from the typical *Graptomyzae*.

Eristalis chalcopygus Wied. Auss. Zw. II, 178 (Manilla). Two ♂, two ♀; Amboina 1873 (*Beccari*).

Syn. **Axona volucelloides** Walk. J. P. Lin. Soc. VII, 213! (Mysol).
Eristalis maxima Dolesch. 2 Bijdr. 29, Tab, X, f. 4! (Amboina).

Axona may be a good genus, but requires a closer definition than that of Walker's.

Eristalis suavissimus Wk. J. Pr. Lin. Soc. III, 95 (Aru). Two ♀, Fly River, N. Guin. Dec. 1875 (*L. M. D'Albertis*). Recognizable ; *E. placens* Wk. (Mysol) also agrees, except legs. I do not find anything about these species in' my notes taken in the Br. Mus.

Eristalis splendens Le Guillou, Rev. Zool. 1842, p. 314-316 ; Macq. D. E. II, 2, 49 (Islds. Salomon).

Syn. **E. cuprcofasciatus** v. d. Wulp, Tijdschr. v. Ent. 1868, 114 (Amboina).
E. metallicus Dol. 2 Bijdr. 30, Tab. X, f. 6 (Amboina).

46 ♀, 15 ♂ from Amboina (*Beccari*, 1873), Hatam, N. Guin. (id. June 1875), Varbusi, Ansus (id. April 1875); Awek, Jobi (Coll Bruijn). Some of the females, chiefly among those from New-Guinea have the velvet-black crossband on the third segment narrower and not angular in front; the same is the case with the crossband on the fourth segment.

Eristalis arvorum (Fab.) Wied. Auss. Zw. II, 184! (Java, China). Two ♀, Kandari, Celebes, April 1874 (*Beccari*).

Eristalis quinquestriatus (Fab.) Wied. Auss. Zw. II, 188! (East-Indies). Two ♂, one ♀; Buitenzorg, Java 1875 (*Ferrari*). The description is not clear in some particulars ; but the type, which I saw in Vienna agrees with my specimen.

Eristalis resolutus Wk. J. Pr. Lin. Soc. III, 95! (Aru; in the Synopsis also N. Guin., Key, Sula).

Four ♀, Aru Islds; Wokan, 1873 (*Beccari*).

The description is recognizable.

Eristalis zonalis (Fab.) Wied. Auss. Zw. II, 152! (China).

SYN. **E. flavofasciatus** Macq. D. E. Suppl. IV, 136 (Java). [Schiner].

One ♀, Mt. Singalang, Sumatra, July 1878 (*Beccari*).

Macquart's description was drawn from a very pale specimen, and must be taken in connection with what he says in the note. The synonymy is admitted as certain by Schiner, Nov. 365, who had received specimens from Paris. In his Suppl. V, 86 Macquart described it a second time, as *Megaspis zonalis* Wied.!

Eristalis errans (Fab.) Wied. Auss. Zw. II, 155! (Java, China).

SYN. **Eristalis varipes** Macq. D. E. II, 2, 46, Tab. X, f. 4 (East-Indies, China).
Eristalis Macquartii Dol. 1 Bijdr, 8, Tab. VII, f. 11
Eristalis Amphicrates Walk. List, etc. III, 623!

Twenty ♂♀ specimens from Buitenzorg, Java, 1875 (*Ferrari*), Sumatra (*Beccari*) and Timor (*L. M. D'Albertis*).

The metallic spots on black ground, on the 3d and 4th abdominal segments are not mentioned in Wiedemann's description, but they exist in the typical specimens.

This is a common and widely distributed species. It also occurs in the Philippine Islands.

Eristalis niger Wied. Auss. Zw. II, 183 (Java).

One ♀, Ramoi, N. Guinea. Febr. 1875 (*Beccari*).

The description agrees very well, only my specimen is smaller; I have not compared it with the type in Vienna. *E. bomboides* Wk. J. Proc. Lin. Soc. IV, 119 ♂ (Celebes) and especially V, 239 ♀ (N. Guinea) may very well be the same species, if we make some allowances for M.r Walker's manner of describing. *E. obscurata* Wk., l. c. V. 239 (N. Guin.), if not the same species, must be closely allied. I have not examined them carefully in the Brit. Mus.

Eristalis multifarius Walk. Ins. Saund. Dipt. 248! (East-Indies).

One ♀, Buitenzorg, Java, 1875 (*Ferrari*).

As I have seen the type in the Br. Mus. I have little doubt that the specimen is a darker variety of the same species. The third abdominal segment is occupied by a large black spot, which leaves only a pale yellow hind margin, and a reddish-yellow triangle in each of the anterior corners; the fourth segment is altogether black, except the yellow hind margin; the four front legs are black, except the proximal half of the tibiae and the root of the tarsi; proximal half of the hind femora ferruginous; a dark reddish ring in the middle of the hind tibiae. Wings strongly tinged with brownish-yellow, except the distal third, which is hyaline. The yellow stripes of the thorax are rubbed off in my specimen.

Eristalis muscoides Walk. J. Pr. Lin. Soc. III, 96! (Aru Isl.ᵈˢ).

One ♂, Amboina 1873 (*Beccari*).

The description agrees tolerably well. In the Brit. Mus. there are two specimens, both with Walker's label; one of them resembles mine in the pattern of the abdomen and the plumose antennae; the other is a different species. *Erist. inscriptus* Dol. resembles this species very much, but has a *bare* arista and the intermediate black spot on segments 3 and 4 is round, instead of wedgeshaped. *E. postscriptus* Walk., l. c. VII, 210 seems to be the same as *inscriptus*; however, I have not compared the types.

Solenaspis nov. gen.

Allied to *Eristalis* and *Pteroptila* Lw. (*Plagiocera* Macq.), but easily distinguished by the shape of its scutellum, by its eyes, which are only subcontiguous in the male, and by its uniformly metallic color.

The scutellum is parallelopidal, its breadth being nearly three times its length; its hind margin is nearly straight in the middle, rounded on the sides only, and the edge is sharp, cut off by a deep groove, running parallel to it.

The glabrous eyes are approximated for a very short distance in the male, but without actual contact, as there is a short, polished, black, linear interval between them; the vertical triangle is nearly twice as long as the above described black linear interval, and the ocelli, placed in its apex, are more distant than usual from the occipital edge. Frontal triangle likewise, unusually long. Antennae inserted on a projection under which the face is hollowed out, as far as the very considerable facial gibbosity above the oral opening. Arista bare. The venation is like that of *Eristalis*, but the anterior crossvein is a little beyond the middle of the discal cell; the surface of the wings is clothed with a dense microscopic pubescence, which is much more distinct here than in *Pteroptila*, and to which the dark color of the wings is chiefly due. The abdomen is rather broad oval; the male hypopygium is concealed under the fourth segment. The hind femora are but slightly incrassated, but the hind tibiae are strongly compressed from the sides and therefore broader, especially on their distal half.

Solenaspis Beccarii n. sp. ♂. Metallic green, shining, with a delicate fulvous pubescence; legs black; wings brown. Length: 14–15 mm.

Face black, with a silvery down, and some yellowish hairs near the eyes; antennae black, arista reddish-brown; front and vertex metallic green; the narrow space separating the eyes (in ♂), black, shining. Thorax metallic green, with a fulvous pubescence, which interferes but little with the lustre of the dorsum; upon the latter, some indistinct purplish stripes are perceptible; on the pleurae, the yellowish hairs almost conceal the metallic ground color. Scutellum metallic green, its posterior edge metallic blue. The yellow pubescence is hardly visible on the metallic green abdomen, except at the base; a side-view shows on the second segment two triangles beset with microscopic fulvous pile (in the place of the ordinary yellow triangles on that segment, so common in the genus *Eristalis*); the two following segments likewise show indistinct patches of that fulvous pile. Legs black; hind femora with a metallic-green reflection; hind tibiae with some blue reflection. Halteres yellow. Tegulae whitish, with a black fringe. Wings brown, with faint subyaline spots in the centre of some of the cells, especially the discal and anal.

Hab. Ramoi, N. Guinea, Febr. 1875 (*Beccari*); a single male.

NB. Plagiocera nitens Bigot, Ann. Soc. Entom. 1880, p. 85 (Dorei, N. Guinea) may be closely related to this species. It cannot well be the same, as the coloring of *S. Beccarii* is green and not coppery, and as the characteristic fulvous pubescence is not mentioned in M.ʳ Bigot's description. The name *Plagiocera* being preoccupied (Klug, Hymen. 1834) should be replaced by *Pteroptila* Loew.

Helophilus bengalensis Wied. (*Eristalis*) Auss. Zw. II, 167, 21 (Bengal)!

One ♀, Buitenzorg, Java, (*Ferrari*).

The last abdominal segment has two yellow spots at the base, not mentioned in the description.

Milesia conspicienda Walk. J. Pr. Lin. Soc. IV, 118 (Celebes).

One ♀, Kandari, Celebes, April 1874 (*Beccari*).

Microdon spec.?

One ♀; Ramoi, N. Guin. Febr. 1875 (*Beccari*).

The specimen was probably immature and the abdomen is very much shrunken. It is a form closely allied to *Microdon*, although the antennae are much shorter and the first posterior cell not divided (however, there is a beginning of such a division on one of the wings). I suspect that this is Walkers *Pa-*

ragus incisuralis or *venosus* (J. Pr. Lin. Soc. VIII, 113, New
Guinea); but I found that out after I had left London and could
not compare the type.

CONOPIDAE.

Conops sp. — Buitenzorg, Java; (*G. B. Ferrari* 1875). — The
description of the coloration of the wings agrees so well with
that of *C. testaceus* Macq. D. E. II, 3, 9 (India), that I am very
much tempted thus to identify it, although *C. testaceus* is a little
larger, and much less dark on thorax and abdomen.

MUSCIDAE CALYPTERAE.

Dexia basifera Walk. J. Pr. Lin. Soc. IV, 130. *Male* (Celebes)!
    Three specimens; Kandari, Celebes, April 1874 (*Beccari*). The
description agrees.

Megistogaster costatus Rond. Ann. Mus. Civ. Gen. VII, (Sa-
rawak, Borneo)!
    One specim., Kandari, Celebes, April 1874 (*Beccari*).
    The type specimen has the posterior crossvein more strongly
bisinuate; the abdomen somewhat reddish-brown; nevertheless
I believe it is the same species. I am doubtful whether it can
be classed with the genus *Megistogaster* Macq., as its abdomen
is very little attenuated at the base and its arista decidedly
plumose, and not merely *tomentose*, as in Macquart's typical
species. The type of *Dexia cylindrica* Wk. J. Pr. Lin. Soc. V,
260 (Celebes) also looks very much like this species, but has
more white at the base of the abdominal segments, as well as
on the pleurae; the face is less prominent, etc.

Stilbomyia prospera Walk. J. Pr. Lin. Soc. IV, 133 (1859)!
(Celebes).

SYN. **Stilbomyia nitidissima** Sn. v. Voll. Versl. en Med. K. Akad. Wet.
1863 (Celebes).
(?) **Spinthemyia fulgida** Bigot, Rev. et Mag. de Zool. 1859 (Celebes).

Two specimens; Kandari, Celebes (*Beccari*).
The abdominal silvery spots are sometimes hardly visible.

Amenia leonina (Fab.) Wied. Auss. Zw. II, 389 (Australia).

SYN. **Amenia imperialis** R. Desv. Myod. 413, 1 (Schiner).
     Ptilostylum albomaculatum Macq. Suppl. IV, 222, Tab. 21, f. 1.
(Schin.).

One ♂; Somerset, Australia, Jan. 1875 (*L. M. D'Albertis*).
The synonymy is after Schiner, Nov. 316, who had types of
Macquart before him. *Rutilia argentifera* Bigot, Ann. S. E. Fr.
1874, 464, is evidently an *Amenia*, but seems to be a different
species.

Rutilia saturatissima Walk. J. Pr. Lin. Soc. V, 287! (Batchian).

Two males; from Andai, N. Guinea (Coll. Bruijn, 1875) and
Ternate (id.).
Description and type agree well.

Rutilia pretiosa Snellen v. Vollenh. Versl. en Med. d. K. Akad. Wetensch. 1863! (Ternate).

SYN. **Rutilia atribasis** Walk. J. Pr. Lin. Soc. V, 287! (Batchian).

One ♀; Andai, N. Guinea (Coll. Bruijn, 1875).
M.ʳ Walker's type has the middle of the black band on the
second segment more drawn out in a triangle or point (which
agrees with the wording of his description), thorax and scutellum are more greenish; nevertheless the identity is hardly
doubtful. I find in my notes that the type of *R. complicita*
Wk. l. c. V, 287 (Batchian) a female, looks very much like
atribasis; the male alongside of it (not mentioned in the description), seemed to be a different species. *R. sapphirina* Walk.
l. c. VI, 9 (Gilolo), looks also like the two above mentioned

species ; but the upper occipital orbit appeared to me narrower, the front likewise etc.

A small female specimen from the Aru Islands (Wokan, 1873, *Beccari*) resembles, *R. pretiosa* very much, and may be a variety. It is only 11 mm. long (the other is fully 16-17 mm.), the coloring although brilliant, is a paler metallic green, the black thoracic stripes are very distinct, but narrow, the second abdominal segment has only a small black triangle in the middle of the hind margin, the remainder of this margin being metallic green ; the pleurae show a large, white hoary spot, below the humeri.

Rutilia mirabilis Guér. Voy. de la Coq. Zool. 297, Tab. 21 , f. 2 (Offak, N. Guinea).

SYN. **Rutilia plumicornis** Macq. D. E. II, 3. 82, Tab. 9, f. 8 (Synonymy in Macq. l. c. l^{er} Suppl. 174).

One ♀, Varbusi, N. Guinea (*Beccari* 1875).

The specimens of this species in the Brit. Mus. (Aru Isl.) have the green stripes on the abdomen more deeply sinuate. *Rut. fervens* Walk. l. c. V, 288 (Batchian) looks very much like this species ; only the abdomen has more reddish coppery reflections.

Rutilia spec. One male ; Gilolo (Coll. Bruijn, 1875). I have not been able to identify it with any description, nor have I seen anything like it in the Brit. Mus.

Echinomyia sp. Four specimens ; Mt. Singalang, Sumatra, July 1878 (*Beccari*).

Prosena pectoralis Wk. J. Pr. Lin. Soc. VII, 226 (Waigiou). One specimen ; Dorei Hum, New Guinea, Febr. 1875 (*Beccari*).

Description vague ; but it agrees as far as it goes ; I did not compare the type.

Idia cervina n. sp. ♂. Thorax yellowish-sericeous, densely covered with black punctures, between which the metallic-greenish ground color is shining through; abdomen black, opaque, the last segment metallic green, shining. Length 8-9 mm.

Face and cheeks black, shining; underside of head fulvous, with fulvous pile; antennae brown, third joint more reddish; arista reddish at the base. The prevailing color of the thoracic dorsum and scutellum is brownish-yellow, produced by a dense sericeousness, or rather pollen, of that color; it is variegated however by dense black punctures, between which the metallic green ground-color of the thorax is faintly shining; short, erect, black hairs, visible from a side view only, cover the thorax. Pleurae with a broad bright fulvous stripe above, clothed with fulvous pile; tegulae also fulvous; pectus metallic blackish-green. Abdomen black, opaque above; the sides and the fourth segment metallic green, shining; venter also metallic green, with black punctures, which extend to the sides. Femora black, tibiae reddish; front tarsi black, first joint reddish; the two posterior pairs reddish-yellow, black at tip. Wings with a yellowish tinge and a brown shadow at the apex, which is darkest near the costa and fades away towards the hind margin.

Hab. Amboina (*Beccari* 1873); six male specimens.

NB. This must be a common species and is probably described before; but I cannot identify it with any species of *Idia*.

Idia xanthogaster Wied. Auss. Zw. II, 349 (Java).

(?) SYN. **Idia australis** Walk. List etc. IV, 809 (Australia) *id.* J. Proc. Lin. Soc. III, 103 (Aru Isl.ᵈˢ) and IV, 132 (Celebes).

One ♂, Amboina, 1873 (*Beccari*); two other ♂ from Yule Islᵈ. N. Guinea (*L. M. D'Albertis*).

The color of the legs (described as black in Wied.) must be variable, because the specimen from Amboina has the base of the tibiae and tarsi brownish-yellow; in the two other specimens they are nearly altogether black. I must have overlooked Wiedemann's type in Vienna, because I find no notice about it among my papers. The type of *australis* Wk. struck me as being the same species; but the description (chest *black* etc.) disagrees in some particulars. — Walker has *xanthogaster* from the Key Islands (1. c. III, 130).

Cosmina prolata Walk. (*Idia*) J. Pr. Lin. Soc. IV, 133! (Celebes).
One ♂, one ♀; Kandari, Celebes, April 1874 (*Beccari*). The description agrees well.

Calliphora bivittata (*Lucilia*) Dolesch. 3de Bijdr. 39 (111) 62 (Amboina).
Two spec., ♂♀; Amboina, Dec. 1874 (*Beccari*). The description agrees perfectly.

Calliphora sp. Dorei Hum, New Guinea, Febr. 1875 (*Beccari*); one ♂.
Resembles *C. papua* Guérin, Voy. de la Coquille, p. 297, very much, but the latter has the base of the abdomen yellow. *Musca calliphoroides* Walk., J. Pr. Lin. Soc. V, 245 (N. Guinea) is perhaps the same as *papua* and comes also very near my species, but the type, which I saw, does not have the black stripe running from the humerus, over the root of the wings to the scutellum, which my specimens show.

Calliphora sp. Dorei Hum, N. Guinea (*Beccari*); one ♀. Very like the preceding, only the legs black.

Ochromyia ferruginea Dol. 2de Bijdr. 38, Tab. X, f. 3! (Amboina).
SYN. **Ochromyia promittens** Walk. J. Pr. Lin. Soc. IV, 134 (Celebes)!

Eleven ♂♀ Ternate 1875; Kandari, Celebes, 1874; Amboina; Ramoi, N. Guinea (*Beccari*).
The extent of the metallic color at the tip of the abdomen is variable; sometimes there is none at all. *Phumosia* (*Ochromyia*) *pallidula* R. Desv. Myod. 427 (Australia) may be the

same species; *Ph. abdominalis* R. D. ibid. (Timor) has much
more green on the abdomen (« les quatre à cinq derniers
segments »); nevertheless M.^{r} v. d. Wulp (Tijdschr. v. Ent.
XXIII), is probably right in taking it for the same species.

Lucilia dux (Esch. Entomogr.) Wied. Auss. Zw. II, 399 (Gua-
ham, Ladrone Islds).

Syn. **Lucilia flaviceps** Macq. D. E. II, 3. 145, Tab. 18, f. 1 (Coromandel,
Pegu).
Chrysomyia Duvaucelii R. Desv. Myod. 451, 19 [v. d. Wulp].

A dozen ♂♀; Aru Islds., Wokan; and Kandari, Celebes
(*Beccari*).

The two first descriptions agree perfectly; moreover, I compared a type of Macquart's in Vienna. Schiner had the species
from Ceylon, the Nicobar Islands and Hongkong. The synonymy
with R. Desvoidy's species is also very probable. — Rondani
(Ann. Mus. Civ. Vol. VII, 425) introduces for this and some
other species the new genus *Compsomyia*.

Lucilia nosocomiorum Dolesch. 2de Bijdr. 37, Tab. III, fig. 5 !
(Amboina).

Two ♂; Amboina (*Beccari*).

Doleschall's description is entirely unmeaning; the word *rood*
(red), in the description of the scutellum must be a misprint
for *rond* (round); I have seen a type in Vienna, which agrees,
with my specimens.

(?) **Pollenia munda** Wied. (*Musca*) Auss. Zw. II, 398 (Java).
One ♂, Java (*Beccari*).

The description agrees, except the « sapphirino resplendens ».
The *Musca viridiaurea* l. c. 397 (Java) the type of which I
saw in Vienna, resembles mine very much; only the tibiae
and tarsi of the latter are yellowish-brown and not metallic-
black; there is a brown shadow near the apex of the wing,
which is also mentioned in the description, but not apparent
in my specimen.

Anisomyia favillacea Walk. J. Pr. Lin. Soc. IV, 135 (Celebes)!
Two specimens; Kandari, Celebes, Apr. 1874 (*Beccari*).
The description is but little intelligible.

Anthomyia albicornis Walk. (*Aricia*) J. Pr. Lin. Soc. VII, 216!
(Mysol).
Two ♂, Dorei Hum, N. Guinea, Febr. 1875 (*Beccari*).
The description is recognizable.

Observation. There are in the collection some 30 or more
species of *Muscidae Calypterae, Dexiae, Tachinae, Luciliae,
Sarcophagae, Anthomyiae,* which I am unable to identify, and
which it would be useless, at present, to describe.

MUSCIDAE ACALYPTERAE.

Sepedon javanensis R. Desv. Myod. 677.
Three specimens; Ajer Manteior and Mt. Singalang, Sumatra,
July, August 1878 (*Beccari*).
I found this species determined in that way in the Museums,
although R. Desvoidy's description does not agree with it very
well.

Micropeza tenuis Dol. 3 Bijdr. 55! (Amboina).
Ramoi, New Guinea, Febr. 1875 (*Beccari*).
Is not a true *Micropeza*, because the second posterior cell is
separated by a crossvein from the discal cell.

Nerius phalanginus Dol. 2 Bijdr. 41 (Java).

Syn. (?) **Nerius fuscus** Wiedem. Auss. Zw. II, 550, Tab. X, f. 2 (Java).
Nerius fuscus (Wied.) Rondani. Ann. M. C. Gen. VII, 411 (Borneo).
(?) **Nerius fuscipennis** Macq. D. E. II, 3, 241, Tab. 32, f. 5 (Java).

Numerous specimens; Kandari, Celebes, April 1874 (*Beccari*).

I give the preference to Doleschall's name, as the most certain.
Wiedemann's description is very far from agreeing, although,

owing to the great difference in size and intensity of coloring
of the specimens, he may mean this species.

Nerius mantoides Walk. J. Proc. Lin. Soc. V, 254! (Dorei, N. Guinea).

SYN. (?) **Nerius tibialis** Dolesch. 2 Bijdr. 52, Tab. III, f. 4! (Amboina).
(?) **Nerius tibialis** (Dol.) Walker, l. c. V, 166 (Amboina).

Two specim.; Mom, N. Guinea (*Beccari* 1875).

Doleschall's description does not quite agree with my specimens; but three types of his which I saw in Vienna were
exactly like them, except that the ends of their tibiae were
infuscated. Walker's description of *N. tibialis* likewise mentions
this character. Walker says about *mantoides* that it can easily
be distinguished from *tibialis* « by its wings », but he leaves us
in the dark about the nature of the difference. Between the
two names I prefer the most certain one.

Nerius inermis Schiner, Novara etc. 248 (Nicobar Islands)!

Eight specimens; Aru Islands, Wokan : Kandari, Celebes
(*Beccari*).

I have seen the type, and the description agrees likewise,
except the color of the palpi, which are yellow in the specimens before me. *Nerius duplicatus* Wied. II, 353 (Java), *Nerius
striatus* Dolesch. (Bijdr. 9, Tab. III, f. 3, Java) are closely allied, if not the same, species. Schiner l. c. observes with good
reason that *Telostylus binotatus* Bigot (Rev. et Mag. de Zool.
1859) seems likewise to belong in the same group. The specimens are very variable in coloring and for this reason it is
hazardous to judge of the identity from mere descriptions. Three
specimens from Hatam, New Guinea, are smaller and darker,
and may perhaps belong to a separate species.

Calobata.

Great difficulties attend the discrimination and identification
of the group of exotic *Calobatae,* characterized by a black body.

with metallic, bluish or greenish, reflections, white front tarsi and wings banded with brown. They are common in the warmer regions of the old and new world; Macquart assumed even the specific identity of some specimens from North-America, Cuba, Java and Australia (*C. albimana* Macq.), and that of *C. tarsata* Wied. (Brazil), with specimens from New-Guinea. Closely resembling species seem to be numerous, and as specimens collected in the same island often agree among themselves in the deviations which they show, it becomes difficult to decide whether to consider them as local varieties or as distinct species. Without attempting to unravel M.[r] Walker's numerous descriptions in this genus, I will characterize five species, which I recognize in the collection before me, and will name three of them, whithout reference to earlier descriptions. None of these species has the well-marked sericeous silvery or golden stripe on the pleurae, in front of the root of the wings, which characterizes some species from the Philippine Islands.

The distance of the posterior crossvein from the apex of the wing is *more than twice* the distance of the end of the second vein to the same apex; wings narrow, with *three* brown crossbands and a brown apex.

tipuloides Walk.

The distance of the posterior crossvein and of the end of the second vein from the apex of the wings is nearly the same; wings with only *one* or *two* brown crossbands, besides the brown apex.

Front coxae and proximal third of front femora yellowish-red : mentum yellow : first posterior cell much coarctate, but not closed ; wings with a single crossband, besides the brown apex ; a velvet black spot on the front, and another one on the vertex, behind the ocelli.

Tip of hind femora red   *albimana* Dol.

Tip of hind femora black   *prudens* n. sp.

Front coxae and front femora black ; mentum black ; first posterior cell closed ; two crossbands on the wings, besides the brown apex; the velvet-black frontal spot is drawn out posteriorly in a point, upon which are the ocelli; the vertex behind this point is metallic, shining.

A narrow, lunate, hyaline crossband begins at the end of the second vein.

lunaria n. sp.

The hyaline crossband at the end of the second vein is as broad as the brown crossband, which precedes it.

morbida n. sp.

Calobata tipuloides Walk., J. Pr. Lin. Soc. VIII, 125. (N. Guin.)!

Two specimens; Ramoi, N. Guinea, Febr. 1875 (*Beccari*).

A well marked species, the description of which in M.ʳ Walker is recognizable.

Calobata albimana Dolesch. (*Taenioptera*) I Bijdr. 11 (413) Tab. 10, f. 4 (Java)!

Twelve specimens from Kandari, Celebes (Apr. 1874), five from Ternate (1875) and two from Ramoi and Soron, N. Guinea (Febr. 1875) all by M.ʳ *Beccari*.

Antennae, including the base of the arista, ferruginous; front and vertex metallic-bluish, shining, except a velvet-black round spot on the front, and a similar spot, of less regular shape, on the vertex; between them, the surroundings of the ocelli have, from a side-view, a whitish reflection. Mentum and palpi reddish-yellow, the latter brownish at the end. Thorax black, with metallic bluish reflections; thinly grayish pollinose, which does not prevent it from being somewhat shining, especially anteriorly and on the scutellum; on the pleurae and pectus, the pollen is more silvery; an opaque black stripe runs from the humerus to the root of the halteres. Abdomen bluish-metallic, more shining at the base than posteriorly; the ovipositor of the same color; hind margins of the intermediate segments reddish (in some specimens this character is not perceptible) ; some erect yellowish hairs on the first segment. Halteres with a black knob. Front coxae and proximal half of the femora yellowish-red; the remainder of the front femora, the tibiae and the base of the first tarsal joint, black; the rest of the front tarsi white. Middle and hind legs yellowish-red ; femora with two, more or less distinct, brown rings, sometimes with an indication of a third one before the tip ; base of hind femora yellowish ; tarsi yellowish, the tips of the joints brown ; the hind tarsi sometimes whitish. Wings with a yellowish tinge ; a brown (not very dark) crossband immediately beyond the anterior crossvein ; it is curved, the concavity being turned towards the apex ; apex brown as far as the end of the second vein. First posterior cell coarctate, and (in most specimens) distinctly open.

NB. The five specimens from Ternate have the frontal velvet-black spot larger ; the fan-like fringe of hairs on the pleurae, above the middle coxae is black, while in the specimens from Celebes and N. Guinea they show, when looked at from the same point of view, a golden reflection.

This is *albimana* Dolesch. (type in Vienna) and not *albimana* Macq. ; the latter must be closely allied, but is represented as having the anal cell much drawn out (Compare Macq. D. E., II, 3, Tab. 33, f. 3). It seems to be the most common species in those regions and will probably be identified with some species described elsewhere. *Cal. albitarsis* Wied., *stylophora* Schin., *macropus* Thoms., *brevicellula* Macq., all belong in the vicinity.

Calobata prudens n. sp. ♂ ♀.

Of the same size as *albimana*, which it resembles exceedingly. The differences principally consist in the color of the tip of middle and hind femora, which is dark brown or black here. The proximal third of the corresponding tibiae is also of a dark color ; their tips are also brown. The third joint of the antennae is brown, instead of ferruginous. The crossband of the wings is straight, or nearly so, on the distal side (and not concave, as in *C. albimana*). The coloring of the body seems to be metallic

greenish, rather than bluish; there seems to be some yellow
on the venter. The comparison of a larger number of well-
preserved specimens would probably disclose other differences.
Hab. Ajer Manteior, Sumatra, August 1878 (*Beccari*); one
♂, two ♀.

Calobata lunaria n. sp. A little smaller than *C. albimana*.
Front metallic blue; the round velvet-black spot is drawn out
posteriorly in a point, which includes the ocelli; beyond this
point the vertex and occiput are metallic-blue, shining. Mentum
and palpi brown; antennal scapus and base of the third joint
reddish, the rest brown (in one of the specimens the whole
antenna is nearly brown). Thorax blackish-blue, thinly whitish
hoary; it is subopaque on the dorsum, where three longitudinal,
linear, blackish, opaque stripes are visible; the pleurae are more
shining. The fan-like row of hairs above the middle coxae is
black. Halteres with a black knob. Abdomen, like the thorax,
of a blackish-blue and whitish hoary color; a smoky black subopaque crossband on the second segment, and a similar, but
broader crossband occupying a considerable portion of segments
3 and 4. Front coxae black, with a bluish reflection and whitish hoary; front legs dark brown; tarsi white from the tip of
the first joint; middle and hind femora dark brown; both with
a narrow reddish ring a short distance before the tip; the extreme base of the hind femora is yellow. Wings with a brown
crossband between the tip of the anal cell and the anterior
crossvein; it becomes evanescent before reaching the posterior
margin; the remainder of the wing, soon beyond the anterior
crossvein, is brown, except a crescent-shaped hyaline spot,
which begins at the end of the second vein and does not quite
touch the posterior margin (at least in fully colored specimens);
this crescent thus cuts off a second, broader crossband, the
rounded sides of which impart to it a somewhat circular appearance. The first posterior cell is closed, and even slightly petiolate.

Hab. Ternate (*Beccari* 1875); four specimens.

NB. 1 have two specimens from Sorong, New Guinea (May 1872, *L. M. D'Albertis*), which resemble *C. lunaria* in every respect (as far as I can discern, because they are indifferently preserved); only the lunate hyaline crossband is replaced here by a much broader one (although not quite as broad as that of *C. morbida*). When Macquart, D. E. II, 3, 245 refers the description of *C. tarsata* Wied. (South America) to a specimen from New Guinea, he probably had such a one before him.

Calobata morbida ♂ ♀, n. sp. Is exceedingly like the preceding species, but differs principally in the coloration of the wings; the intermediate brown crossband is much narrower, in consequence of which the hyaline interval between it and the apical spot is broader, (as broad as the crossband); thus it comes that the end of the second vein is here on hyaline ground, while it is on brown ground in *C. lunaria*. The antennae are darker than in *lunaria* (altogether dark brown or black, only the base of the arista reddish), the hind legs, on the contrary less dark, (the hind femora are reddish-brown, or in some specimens, brownish red, the whole distal third is of a ligther, reddish shade, with an indication of a brownish ring, a little before the tip; at the base of the femora some yellow is visible, but not in all the specimens). The blackish thoracic stripes have a different shape, the lateral ones not being linear, but triangularly expanded in the middle and connected with a blackish pattern on both sides of the thoracic suture.

Torax of
Calobata morbida.

Hab. Buitenzorg, Java (*G. B. Ferrari*, 1875); Ajer Mantcior and Kaju Tanam, Sumatra (August and Sept. 1878, *Beccari*). A dozen specimens.

Nestima nov. gen.

Nestima has the characters of *Calobata*, but is especially distinguished by the peculiar structure of the metanotum: under the triangular scutellum there is a conical projection of the

upper portion of the metanotum, which looks like a second
scutellum. The body is more slender than that of *Calobata;* the
anterior part of the thorax, from a side-view, has the shape of
a cone; the legs are more slender than in *Calobata* and the
middle and hind femora are longer; the very long middle femora have some minute spines on the underside, towards the
tip; on the hind femora the spines are almost imperceptible.
Venation of *Calobata;* but first posterior cell much less coarctate
towards the end; the end of the second vein is more than
twice as near the apex of the wing as the posterior crossvein
(the venation, in this respect, is like that of *Calobata tipuloides*
Wk.). — The ventral forklike appendage of the male has rather long prongs; the male genitals are comparatively small;
the ovipositor is tubular, short and does not differ much in
appearance from the preceding segment.

Nestima polita n. sp. ♂ ♀. Dark brown, shining, wings uniformly tinged with brown. Length 12-13 mm.

Head brown, shining; front yellowish-red, with an opaque
black spot in the middle; antennae brownish-red; upper edge
of the third joint brown; arista pubescent; palpi brownish.
Thorax uniformly dark brown, shining. Abdomen brown, but
less dark than the thorax. Halteres with a yellow knob, stem
brown. Front femora and coxae brownish red, the femora with
a pale brown ring before the tip; front tibiae brown in the
middle; the base yellowish, the tip whitish; front tarsi yellowish-white; two last joints brown. Middle legs reddish brown,
the tibiae and tarsi darker. Hind legs brownish-red; tip of
tibiae and the tarsi brown. Wings with a uniformly brown
tinge. First posterior cell broadly open.

Hab. Andai, N. Guinea, Aug. 1872 (*L. M. D'Albertis*); Hatam, N. Guinea, July 1875 (*Beccari*). — Two ♂, one ♀.

Trypeta quadrifera Walk. (*Helomyza*) J. Pr. Lin. Soc. V, 246! (Dorei, N. Guinea).

A ♂ and a ♀; Andai, N. Guinea, 1872 (*L. M. D'Albertis*); Hatam, ibid. June 1875 (*Beccari*).

The description agrees well; *Helom. optatura* Wk. l. c. VIII, 116 (N. Guin.) is exceedingly like this species, and differs only in the shape of the black spots of the abdomen. The large scutellum bears six bristles, the arista is plumose, the frontal bristles large and conspicuous; there is a strong bristle on the cheeks, under the eye, on each side.

Trypeta stellipennis Walker, J. Pr. Lin. Soc. IV, 159! (Celebes).

SYN. **Sophira punctifera** Wk., J. Pr. Lin. Soc. VI, 15! (Gilolo).

Twelve ♂♀ specim., from Ternate and Kandari, Celebes, April 1874 (*Beccari*). Although it is said in the description of *Sophira punctifera* that the antennal arista is bare, it is distinctly plumose in the typical specimen, which I have seen in the Br. Mus. Scutellum with six bristles, third vein pubescent. Comes nearest to the genus *Eutreta* Lw.

Trypeta melaleuca Walk. J. Pr. Lin. Soc. VII, 238! (North Ceram).

SYN. **Trypeta Atilia** Walk. List etc. III, 1021 (China).

One ♂, two ♀, Kandari, Celebes, April 1874 (*Beccari*).

M.ʳ W.'s description agrees well. I have the same species from the Philippines (Prof. C. Semper). *Tryp. quadrincisa* Wied. is very like this species, at least the specimens so determined by Schiner in Vienna (Nicobar Islands); only the small intermediate dot on the hind margin is absent. Schiner places it in the genus *Acidia*, and I think he is right.

Trypeta signifacies Walk. J. Pr. Lin. Soc. V, 165! (Amboina) *Male.*

One ♀, Ternate 1875 (*Beccari*).

I have seen the type which seemed to be the same species ;
nevertheless, the description, which I compared later, disagrees
in some particulars. Legs black; tarsi white except the two
last joints, which are black. Abdomen metallic blackish green.
A white streak on each side of the thorax between the root of
the wings and the humeri. Front brown, whitish-yellow along
the eyes ; posterior orbits yellowish white. Third antennal joint
whitish, its upper edge brown ; basal joints black. Face brownish black, with whitish spots, a pair of which, on the oral
margin, are especially conspicuous. Palpi white.

Trypeta spec. — Aru Islands (Wokan), 1873 (*Beccari*). One ♀.
It is an *Urellia* with two bristles on the scutellum ; wing-
pattern very like that of *U. gnaphalii* Lw., without being ab-
solutely identical. The european *U. stellata* Lw., or a species
undistinguishable from it, occurs in Australia, according to
Loew.

Dacus emittens Walk. J. Pr. Lin. Soc. IV, 152 ! (Celebes).
Three ♂♀, Kandari, Celebes, April 1874 (*Beccari*).
The description agrees only tolerably.

Dacus conformis Walk. (*Strumeta*) J. Pr. Lin. Soc. I, 33, Tab.
II, f. 4 ! (Singapore).
One ♂, two ♀; Kandari, Celebes, Apr. 1874 (*Beccari*).
Description and figure agree. The specimen of *D. fascipennis*
Wied. (Java) in the Winthem collection in Vienna has the
same coloration of the wings ; the abdomen of the specimen is
soiled, but the description proves it to be different from my
specimens. *Bactrocera fasciatipennis* Dolesch. I Bijdr. Tab. III,
f. 1, (Java) of which I have also seen a type in Vienna, likewise agrees with my specimens in the pattern of the wings ; but
the body is differently colored.

Dacus Ritsemae Weyenb. Archives Néerl. T. IV (Java).
One ♂; Amboina, (*Beccari*).

Description and figure agree quite well, except that the tibiae are described as darker towards the tip.

Dacus (?) **furcifer** Walker, J. Pr. Lin. Soc. VI, 14! (Gilolo). One ♂; Ternate, *Beccari*.
The description is recognizable; it is a *Trypetid*, but not a *Dacus*. The pattern of the wings is very like that of a *Cleitamia*.

Dacus (?) **mutilloides** Walk. J. Pr. Lin. Soc. III. 115! (Aru). One spec.; Fly River, N. Guin. Dec. 1875 (*L. M. D'Albertis*). The description says « halteres whitish », while in my specimen the knob is brown; the distance between the two crossveins is described as larger, than I find it. The type in the Br. Mus. is smaller, but seems to belong to the same species. It is not a *Dacus*, and apparently not a *Trypetid* at all; but the specimen is too badly preserved for study.

Themara (Acanthoneura?) maculipennis Westw. Cabin. Oɤ. Entom. p. 38, Tab. 18, f. 4 (*Achias*).

SYN. **Achias Horsfieldi** Westw. Trans. Ent. Soc. V, 1850, Tab. 23, f. 9. (♂).
Themara ampla Walker, Journ. Proc. Lin. Soc. 1856, Vol. I, p. 33, Tab. 1, f. 5 (♀) (the synonymy is acknowledged by Walker himself, l. c. pag. 134).

M.ʳ Westwoods specimen was from Java. M.ʳ Walker's were from Borneo and Singapore, and the one before me is from Sungei Bulu, Sumatra (*Beccari*, Sept. 1878). Doleschall (3ᵈᵉ Bijdr. 52) had it from Amboina. Besides the pale colored base of the abdomen, there is a pale colored crossband, not mentioned in M.ʳ Westwood's description. The female, described and figured in Walker, has *two* such crossbands. The specific identity is not in the least doubtful.

Generically, this species has nothing to do with *Achias*. It is a *Trypeta* and may very well belong in the genus *Acanthoneura* Macq. D. E. II, 3, 220, on account of its bristly costa, first and third veins, bisinuate second vein, structure of antennae, coloring etc. — Until this is proved however, the name *Themara* may remain for it.

Trypeta (Acanthoneura) polyxena n. sp. ♀. Wings brown, with several hyaline spots; apex with a well defined yellow segment. Length: 7-8 mm.

Head, including the antennae, brownish-yellow; frontal stripe more reddish; bristles black. Thorax brownish-yellow, with some faintly-marked brownish stripes; metanotum black on the sides; abdomen black, two basal segments yellow, the second with a black band in the middle. Halteres and legs brownish-yellow. Wings brown with the following white spots: a triangle on the costa at the end of the first vein; a small round spot about the middle of the first post. c.; a larger, oval spot in the discal cell, almost under the small crossvein; a triangle on the hind margin, in the second post. c.;

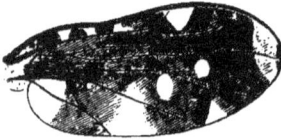

Acanthoneura polyxena.

a subhyaline band reaches across the third post. c. into the discal, where it becomes yellowish; two small subhyaline spots, coarctate in the middle, in the costal cell, inside of the auxiliary vein; a yellowish spot immediately beyond this vein; and finally, a well defined yellow segment forming the apex of the wing, within which, at the tip of the third vein, there is a small brown spot.

Hab. Java (*Beccari*, 1874); one female.

NB. This species agrees with the characters of *Acanthôneura* Macq. D. E. II, 3, 220: bristly costa, first and third veins, undulated second vein; arista plumose etc. The typical species, *A. fuscipennis*, from Bengal, is even very like *polyxena* in the distribution of the spots on the wings, but Macquarts description and figure are too indefinite. My only specimen is very much denuded of thoracic macrochetae; still I can see by the scars, that there were four of them on the scutellum. The third antennal joint is longer than broad, with nearly parallel sides, the front side being a little concave, the tip rounded ; the hairs on the arista moderately long. The anal cell is drawn out in a point ; the first vein ends a little beyond the anterior crossvein ; the second forms two waves and then turns upwards towards the margin; the third almost straight, with very slight sinuosities; strongly diverging from the fourth ; the fourth slightly arched before the posterior crossvein, thus expanding the discal cell a little ; crossveins nearly straight and perpendicular ; the posterior one with a very slight sinuosity in the middle. Macquart's figure (Tab. 30, f. 2) is only an approximation. The ovipositor is flat, triangular, very broad at base and comparatively long. *Ptilona* v. d. Wulp (Tijdschr. etc. XXIII) resembles *Acanthoneura* somewhat in the coloration of the wings, but differs in the absence of bristles on the veins, in the more straight course of the second vein etc.

Xiria obliqua n. sp. ♂. Wings with a brown apex and an oblique brown crossband, both coalescing near the posterior margin. Length 9-10 mm.

Head, proboscis and palpi black ; a purplish reflection on the large transverse facial swelling ; vertex, and two stripes running down from it, metallic blue, shining. Antennae black ; third joint pale yellow, with a whitish reflection near the base ; arista plumose. Thorax including scutellum metallic blue, with purple reflections ; but little shining ; its surface is finely chagreened and pubescent ; pectus blackish, with a whitish, sericeous pubescence. Halteres yellow. Abdomen metallic purple, blue towards the end. Coxae and femora pale yellow; tip of the latter brown ; tibiae and front tarsi black; first and base of second joint of middle tarsi whitish, the remainder black ;

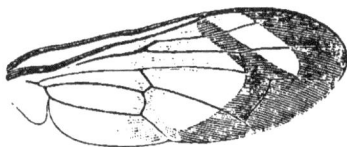

Xiria obliqua.

the hind tarsi have the same color, only the first joint is more yellowish. The wings have the apex brown, which color extends

along the posterior margin nearly as far as the tip of the sixth
vein, where the brown becomes much fainter ; an oblique brown
crossband begins at the end of the first vein, runs over the
oblique anterior crossvein and ends in coalescing with the
brown of the posterior margin ; thus, between crossband and
the brown apex, an oblique hyaline crossband is formed,
which does not reach the fourth vein; the base of the wing is
nearly hyaline about as far as the proximal end of the submarginal cell ; the interval between this and the brown oblique
crossband has a brownish-yellow tinge.

Hab. Mt. Singalang, Sumatra, July 1878 (*Beccari*).

NB. I refer this species to the genus *Xiria* Walk. J. Pr. Lin.
Soc. I, 36, Tab. II, f. 2. *Xiria antica* Wk. (Mt. Ophir) resembles *X. obliqua* in the sculpture and coloring of the body, and
differs principally in the coloration of the wings, the brown
stripe not running obliquely and not being connected with the
apical spot. A third species of the same genus seems to be the
Trypeta violacea Wied. Auss. Zw. II, 476 (Java), which also
has the same coloring of the body, but again differs in the
shape of the brown spots on the wings. The three species have
the same coloring of the legs, except that *X. obliqua* has the
front tarsi black.

I will now enumerate some characters of the genus, in ad-
dition to those which are visible on M.r Westwood's figures of
X. antica.

Xiria has the auxiliary vein closely approximated to the first
longitudinal vein, with a very obsolete connection between its
end and the costa ; in this respect it resembles *Trypeta*. But I
do not perceive the row of bristles on the front, near the orbit,
characteristic of *Trypeta*. There are two large bristles on the
vertex, one each side, near the upper corner of the eye, and a
similar pair a little lower on the front; a very weak pair of
erect bristles is perceptible near the ocelli, one on each side ;
(*X. antica* is either different in this respect, or the figure 2 *b*,
in Walker, l. c., has too many bristles). The front between

the antennae and the second pair of bristles is clothed with scattered, minute hairs. This distribution of bristles is not that of *Trypeta*. The face is very characteristic ; a large transverse swelling a little below its middle , produces a very projecting profile (see the figure 2 *a* in Walker, l. c.). The third antennal joint of *Xiria obliqua* is a little shorter than that of *X. antica* (if rendered correctly in the figure l. c. 2 *c*). The scutellum has six bristles : six other strong macrochetae are inserted on each side of the thoracic dorsum, and a weaker seventh bristle just above each corner of the scutellum. I do not perceive any mesothoracic bristle on the pleurae nor a prothoracic one above the front coxae ; both in the meaning of Loew, Monogr. etc. III, 33. The costa and the first vein are rather densely hairy ; the third vein is beset with scattered hairs, visible under a strong lens; the fifth vein bears some strong hairs before the crossveins, closing the basal cells.

The ovipositor of *X. violacea* is described by Wiedemann as « breit umgeschlagen », whatever that may mean.

Stenopterina eques Schiner, Novara etc. 288 (Stuart Island).

SYN. **Michogaster bambusarum** Dolesch. I Bijdr. II (413), Tab. 8. f. 3 !
(Java).
Stenopterina abrupta Thoms. Eug. Resa, 578 [v. d. Wulp.].
Stenopterina labialis Rondani , Ann. Mus. Civ. Gen. 1875 , 430 !
(Borneo).

Two ♀; Ternate 1875 (*Beccari*); Amboina 1874 (*id.*).

D.ʳ Schiner's description agrees exactly with my specimen. Doleschalls is too short for identification ; but I saw a type of his in Vienna. The antennal arista is pubescent at the base only, and Doleschall's expression « seta plumosa » somewhat misleading. The species agrees with the characters of the genus, as given by Loew in the Monogr. of N. Am. Dipt. III, 96.

Stenopterina didyma n. sp. ♀ . Wings with a large apical brown spot, and a brown, round spot on each of the two crossveins. Length 7 mm.

Face black, shining below, as well as the clypeus; whitish
hoary under the antennae; inner orbits of the eyes also white.
Front blackish-blue; the front above the antennae rather convex.
Antennae: basal joints reddish; third joint more or less brown.
Occiput black, with a gray pollen below, near the orbits.
Thorax greenish-blue; a distinct gray stripe in the middle of
the dorsum. Pleurae grayish-sericeous, except a shining metallic-
green spot in the middle. Femora dark metallic green, with
yellowish-brown ends, tibiae brownish, the front pair darker;
tarsi brownish, paler at base; front tarsi nearly black. Halteres
yellowish. Abdomen metallic blue, with
violet reflections; last segment metallic
green. Wings subhyaline; stigma dark
brown; apex with a large brown spot
between the costa and the fourth vein,
but encroaching very little beyond the
latter; a round brown spot on the anterior crossvein, and a somewhat smaller one on the posterior crossvein; these three
brown marks are large enough to come very near each other,
without being in contact.

Stenopterina didyma

Hab. Hatam, N. Guinea, June 1875 (*Beccari*); three females.

NB. This species differs in its characters from the typical
Stenopterinae. As in *S. eques,* the third and fourth veins are con-
verging; the transverse thoracic depression is arcuate and unin-
terrupted, but the second vein ends in the costa at a rounded,
instead of an acute angle; the anterior crossvein is *not oblique;*
the posterior one is slightly sinuate; the thorax is less bulky
and its vertical diameter shorter; the front coxae are shorter.

Stenopterina chalybea Dolesch. (*Herina*), 3de Bijdr. 53 (Amboina).

Four ♂, seven ♀. — Amboina, Dec. 1874; Ternate 1875;
Kandari, Celebes, April 1874; Dorei Hum, N. Guinea, Febr.
1875 (*Beccari*).

Doleschall's short description agrees well, except that the tips
of the femora, in my specimens, are reddish. Schiner's *S. ba-*

taviensis (Novara, 288) may be the same species, only its legs are less dark, which is also the case with one of my specimens. The extent and intensity of the brown color on the wings is variable; the specimens from New Guinea have most of it.

NB. This species differs from the typical *Stenopterinae* in several important characters and may constitute a separate genus : the scutellum has six bristles, instead of four ; the interrupted sutures on both sides of the mesothorax are not connected by a depression running across the latter ; the thorax is less bulky ; the stigma is shorter, the front coxae likewise; the small crossvein is oblique (as in *S. eques*), but the fourth vein does not converge with the third (rather diverges from it). The gutterlike (ovipositor-bearing) fifth abdominal segment of the female, protruding from under the fourth, is longer here, and therefore more conspicuous.

Stenopterina (?) sp. One ♂ Kandari, Celebes, April 1874 (*Beccari*).

Resembles *Dacus obtrudens* Wk. J. Pr. Lin. Soc. III, 117 (Aru Isl.ᵈˢ) very much, but, as far as I can judge from a note taken about the type, the coloration of the wings of the latter is exactly like the preceding species, while in the present one, the brown cloud on the posterior crossvein runs across the penultimate section of the fourth vein and includes the anterior crossvein. Generically, the specimen belongs in the same group with the preceding species; although most of the bristles of the scutellum are broken, I can see the scars of six.

Cleitamia astrolabei Boisduval, Faune de l' Océanie, 668 (*Ortalis*). Macquart, H. N. Dipt. II, 440, Tab. 19, fig. 4 ; id. Dipt. Exot. II, 3, 204, Tab. 27, f. 7.

Van der Wulp, Tijdschr. etc. XI, Tab. IV, f. 12.

SYN. **Poticara triarcuata** Walk. J. Pr. Lin. Soc. V, 248 (Dorei, N. Guin.).

Twelve ♂, two ♀; Ramoi, N. Guin. June 1872 (*L. M. D'Albertis*); Febr. 1875 (*Beccari*); Hatam, N. Guinea, June 1875 (id.).

The head of the male varies in breadth ; there are specimens, in which it is as broad as the thorax is long. In the female the breadth of the head also varies, but not as much as in the male.

Cleitamia liturata n. sp. ♂ ♀.

This species is exceedingly like *C. amabilis* in the coloration of body and wings ; but the antennae are darker, the halteres yellow (instead of black); the apex of the wings has no other brown border but that, naturally formed by the brown color of the costal vein ; the brown pattern on the proximal half of the wing is different, the space between the costa and the fifth vein not being entirely filled out with brown. The venation is different ; the second vein does not form that bold curve upwards, to come in contact with the first before its tip, and then gradually merge in the costa, but takes the ordinary course, with gentle sinuosities, and ends in the costa a little beyond the tip of the first vein. The structure of the costa *in the male* is very peculiar : there is a distinct depression or sinus about the middle of the anterior margin, in consequence of which the costa comes almost in contact with the first vein, the latter being free at both ends only. The costa shows, at its proximal end, a peculiar swelling about 2 mm. long., with an abrupt, rounded ending, and a cross-suture before the middle; it is clothed with a microscopic pubescence.

Hab. One ♂, one ♀, Ramoi, N. Guinea, Febr. 1875 (*Beccari*).

Cleitamia amabilis n. sp. ♂. — Face yellowish, opaque, more reddish above, silvery below the antennae ; front dark brown or black, subopaque, with a velvet-black angular crossband above the antennae; on each side of this band the orbit of the eye is silvery ; upper part of the front on each side with a round, opaque, velvety spot ; above these spots, the vertex is metallic-blue ; posterior orbits silvery. Antennae brown ; third joint reddish-yellow; arista brown, short-plumose, yellow at base. Thorax reddish-brown, darker in front, opaque : pleurae with a

sericeous down, more distinct posteriorly. Abdomen shining-black, with greenish-metallic reflections, clothed with a microscopic, whitish pubescence (distinct from a side view only), and with half a dozen stiff, long bristles at the tip (in the ♂). Halteres black. Legs black; femora, except the ends, yellow; front coxae yellow. Wings: a large triangular brown spot occupies the whole proximal half; the apex of the (inverted) triangle is near the hind margin, without touching it; the base rests on the costa; within the triangle there is a triangular hyaline spot, also resting on the costa, and leaving only a narrow stripe of brown between it and a coarctate hyaline crossband, crossing the middle of the wing (in some specimens it is interrupted in the middle). Beyond this hyaline crossband, a broad brown one, expanded in the middle, reaches from the costa to the posterior margin; between it and the apex, the space is hyaline, except that the costa has a narrow, but well-defined brown edge, of perfectly equal breadth, which almost reaches the end of the fourth vein. Length 8-9 mm.

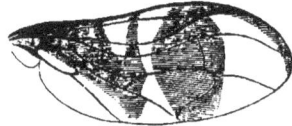

Cleitamia amabilis.

Hab. Hatam, New Guinea (*Beccari* 1875); seven male specimens.

Cleitamia rivellioides n. sp. ♀. — Head very much like that of *C. amabilis* in coloring, only the face darker, reddish brown, with strong bluish-metallic reflections; more reddish above, and silvery under the antennae; orbits silvery, especially on both sides of the antennae and posteriorly; front black or brownish-black, subopaque; a velvet black crossband above the antennae and a pair of velvety spots higher up, before the vertex; the latter metallic-blue. Antennae reddish or reddish-brown, arista short-plumose. Thorax reddish-brown posteriorly, darker anteriorly, opaque; an opaque brown, oblique stripe on each side alongside of the thoracic suture; pleurae reddish-brown, with bluish, metallic reflections and slightly sericeous. Abdomen black,

with a slight bluish-metallic lustre and a microscopic, whitish,
erect pubescence. Halteres black. Legs black; femora yellow,
except their ends; front coxae
yellow. Wings sub-hyaline, with
brown crossbands, not unlike those
of a *Rivellia:* the first, nearest to
the base, runs obliquely through
the second basal cell, along the
fifth vein, and before reaching the
end of the latter turns towards the posterior margin (inside
of the 3ᵈ post. c.); the second, in the shape of a small inverted
triangle, coalesces at its base with the brownish-yellow costal
cells, fills out the proximal end of the marginal cell, where it
is more yellowish-brown, and includes a hyaline spot, and touches
with its apex the first band; the third band, about the middle
of the wing, likewise ends in the first band, at the very point
where the latter turns off from the fifth vein; the fourth covers
both crossveins and is prolonged along the costa nearly as far
as the fourth vein, in the shape of a narrow brown edge of
equal breadth, thus forming a regular half a circle. Length
about 8 mm.

Cleitamia rivellioides.

Hab. Hatam, N. Guinea (*Beccari,* 1875); seven females.

Euxesta prima n. sp. ♀. — Head, including the antennae,
brownish-red; face but little excavated; antennae rounded;
arista bare; vertex black. Thorax and abdomen metallic-green.
Halteres yellow. Legs black; front coxae and knees reddish;
first joint of hind and middle tarsi
brownish-yellow (in some specimens
nearly brown). Wings hyaline, with
the following brown marks; the costal
cell is infuscated from the root up to
a littte beyond the humeral crossvein;
the stigma is brown, as well as a nearly square spot between
it and the fourth vein; this spot does not include the anterior
crossvein; a brown spot at the apex of the wing is bounded

Euxesta prima

posteriorly by the fourth vein; on the proximal side, its boundary does not quite reach the middle of the last section of the fourth vein.

Hab. Kandari, Celebes, April 1874 (*Beccari*). Six females.

NB. Hitherto the genus *Euxesta* was represented by species from America only. *E. prima* is very like the North-American species of the genus in its general appearance and answers the description of the generic characters as given in the Berl. Entom. Zeitschr. 1867, p. 297, and in the Monographs of the North Amer. Dipt. III, p. 153; only the front is a little more convex and the face less excavated than in *E. notata* Wied. The venation and coloration of the wings is very like l. c. Tab. IX, f. 10, only the apical spot fully reaches the fourth vein, but is less broad; the spot under the stigma is smaller.

Rhadinomyia orientalis Schiner, Novara etc. 290! (Java).

Three specimens; top of Mt. Pangerango in Java, 1874 (*Beccari*).

Add to Schiner's description a narrow brown crossband starting from the first longitudinal vein and running across the proximal end of the submarginal cell to the proximal end of the discal. I failed to notice in Vienna, whether Schiner's types have that crossband. The genus belongs, I believe to the *Ulidina*, but the posterior angle of the anal cell is *not* drawn out in a point.

Platystoma punctiplena Walk. J. Pr. Lin. Soc. V, 268! (Celebes).

SYN. **Platystoma stellata** Wk. l. c. I, 32 (Malacca)!
Platystoma atomaria Wk. l. c. IV, 148 (Celebes)!
Platystoma parvula Schiner, Nov. etc. 286 (Batavia)!

Three specimens; Kandari, Celebes, April 1874 (*Beccari*).

Pl. parvula Schin., which I saw in Vienna, seems to be the same species, some discrepancies of the description notwithstanding.

Lamprogaster lepida Walk. Tr. Ent. Soc. N. S. IV, 226 ! (Celebes) agrees exactly with mine in the coloring of the wings; but the body is metallic-green, head and legs reddish. It may be nevertheless the same species as mine; by all means, I would not describe the single specimen I have as a new species when there are so many closely related and conflicting species. *L. luteipennis* (Celebes), Walk. J. Pr. Lin. Soc. V, 261, seems to be the same species as *L. lepida. L. sepsoides* Wk. is closely allied, but has more hyaline wings.

Kandari, Celebes, April 1874 (*Beccari*); one specimen.

Lamprogaster spec. Kapaor, N. Guinea, April 1872 (*L. M. D'Albertis*); one specimen.

This species has nearly the same distribution of the spots on the wings as the preceding; but it is much smaller, the wings are more hyaline; the legs are black and only the first joint of the tarsi reddish, but clothed with a dense whitish microscopic pubescence which, in a certain light, makes them appear white. I did not have this specimen with me in London and could not therefore name it.

Lamprogaster costalis Walk. J. Proc. Lin. Soc. V, 247 (Dorei, New Guinea)!

The description is recognizable, although Walker, as usual, calls the yellowish wings « cinereous ».

Dorei, N. Guinea, Dec. 1875, *Beccari.* Two specimens.

Lamprogaster superna Wk. (Gilolo) and *quadrilinea* (Aru), seem to be closely allied to *L. costalis.*

Lamprogaster sp. — Aru Isl.[ds], Wokan (*Beccari* 1873).

One somewhat immature specimen. The wings are yellowish, without any spots; the legs reddish.

Euprosopia potens Walk. (*Platystoma*) J. Pr. Lin. Soc. VI, 12! (Gilolo, Ternate).

Ternate, 1875 (*Beccari*); two specimens (♂ ♀).

Euprosopia fusifacies Walk. J. Pr. Lin. Soc. III, 113! (Aru). One ♀, Fly River, N. Guinea, 1876-77 (*L. M. D'Albertis*). The specimen does not quite agree with the description (especially the head, which seems however spoiled by moisture), nevertheless the identity is not doubtful.

Euprosopia tigrina n. sp. ♂. Black, thorax, with longitudinal bright yellow stripes, abdomen with one such stripe; wings with three brown crossbands on their distal half; apex brown, coalescent with the third crossband. Long. corp. 8 mm.

Face and front brownish-red: cheeks and orbits of the eyes silvery; palpi dark brown, reddish at base; antennae brownish-red; arista black, reddish at base, short-plumose on its proximal third only. Thorax black, with five fulvous stripes; one in the middle of the dorsum, running from the collare to the end of scutellum; one each side between the humerus and the lateral corner of the scutellum (without encroaching upon the latter): one each side across the pleurae; these stripes, especially the three middle ones, have perfectly parallel sides. Pectus grayish hoary in the middle, which color also invades the coxae. Abdomen black above, with a longitudinal pale yellow dorsal stripe, of equal breadth; male genitals black; venter grayish. Legs black;

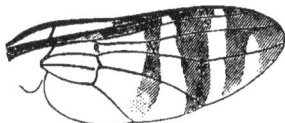

Euprosopia tigrina.

first tarsal joints white, their tip black. Wings subhyaline; the distal half with three blackish-brown crossbands, attenuated behind, separated by very narrow intervals along the costa; apex black, coalescent on the costa with the third band.

Hab. Dorei, N. Guinea, Novemb. 1875 (*Beccari*); one male.

Achias Albertisi n. sp. ♂. Very like the *A. longividens* Wk.; differs principally in the direction of the brown lines of the face and in the posterior crossvein not being clouded with brown. Length 11-12 mm.

The breadth of the head from end to end of the oculiferous

peduncles is 20 mm. in the largest and 14 in the smallest of the five specimens before me. The peduncles are dark brown, the eyes yellowish; the concave front between the peduncles is also brown, but shows two rounded brownish-yellow spots, which vary in size in different specimens; some yellow marks between these spots are less distinct, and, in most specimens, invisible. The lower part of the head (below a line connecting the peduncles and passing over the root of the antennae) is yellow; a brown stripe issues from the underside of the brown peduncle, crosses the face, strikes the middle of the antennal furrow, and, filling it out, reaches the oral margin very near the end of the corresponding stripe on the opposite side. Thus, the interval of the antennal furrows remains yellow; it only shows a brown spot in its *upper* part, near the root of the antennae. All my specimens agree in this coloration of the face and head, while that of *A. longividens* Walk. J. Pr. Lin. Soc. III, 121 (Aru Islands) is exactly as M.ʳ Westwood figures it in the Trans. Ent. Soc. Lond. N. S. V, Tab. 13, f. 4-5 (1861); that is, the brown stripes, connecting the horns or peduncles with the edge of the mouth do *not* fill out the antennal grooves, the bottom of which is, for this reason, yellow, but remain on the side of them; in the *lower* part of the yellow space between the grooves, there is an elongated brown spot; the concave front is much more yellow than it *A. longividens*. These differences seem to be constant; they have decided me to consider my specimens as specifically distinct; to them may be also added that *A. Albertisi* has no brown cloud on the posterior crossvein, and that its scutellum is less metallic green than that of the other species. A closer comparison would probably disclose other differences; but at present, I have no specimens of *A. longividens* before me.

Antennae brown, arista yellowish at base; palpi brownish yellow. Thorax brownish-black; on the dorsum there are five yellowish-sericeous stripes; the two lateral ones and the middle one are broader, the latter expanding triangularly in front of the scutellum; the two remaining, intermediate stripes, are mere lines and do not reach the scutellum. Scutellum blackish-metallic green, opaque. Abdomen metallic green, shining, with some purple reflections; the base is more or less yellowish, with yellowish hairs. Legs black; proximal half of the front and middle femora yellow. The wings have a brown margin along the costa, which sends out a short branch, covering the anterior crossvein; the rest of the wing is tinged with pale brownish-yellow; the first basal cell and a small space on the distal side of the anterior crossvein, are more hyaline.

Hab. Hatam, New Guinea, September 1872 (*L. M. D'Albertis*). Five male specimens.

Achias latividens Walk. l. c. III, 121 (♀) and VII, 229 (♂?) (Aru Isl.^{ds} and Waigiou); Westwood, l. c. fig. 6.

One ♀; Andai, New Guinea, August 1872 (*L. M. D'Albertis*). Agrees with Mr Westwood's figure, as well as with a male specimen, communicated to me by G. H. Verral Esq., in the direction of the brown stripes on the face and in the coloration of the wings. The whole apex, as far as the posterior crossvein, is slightly tinged with brown; the crossvein itself is but a little darker. The horns of the male are about half as long as in *longividens*, to which, otherwise this species bears the closest resemblance.

Achias dacoides Walk. J. Pr. Lin. Soc. VIII, 133! (*Salwatti*) ♀.

SYN. **Achias aspiciens** Walk. l. c. VII, 229! (Waigiou) ♂.

One ♀, Dorei Hum, *Beccari*, Febr. 1875.

I believe that both species, described by Mr Walker, are synonymous, and that the specimen before me belongs to the same species. The types show some reddish stripes on the thorax, which are also mentioned in the description, but which do not exist in my specimen. Although this species is much more slender than the others, and although its tegulae are smaller, the structure of the head and of the anal cell prove its close relationship to the typical species. I prefer the name *dacoides* as the description agrees better with my specimen, which is of the same sex with M.ʳ Walker's type.

Note on the genus Achias. Since Fabricius described as *Achias oculatus* (Syst. Antl. 1805) a single specimen brought by Bosc from Java, no true *Achias* seems to have reached Europe (at least there is none on record), until M.ʳ Wallace rediscovered this genus in the Aru Islands and in New Guinea. Macquart gave, it is true, a description of *A. oculatus* (Hist. Nat. Dipt. II, 260; 1835) « d'après un individu du Cabinet de M.ʳ Robyns à Bruxelles », but in Dipt. Exot. II, 3, 158 (1843) he never mentions this specimen; on the contrary, he says that the fabrician type is « le seul individu connu ». Upon comparison it becomes evident that the description in the Hist. Nat. Dipt. is but a paraphrase of the very inexact description in Robineau Desvoidy's Myodaires, p. 433.

The two species described and figured by M.ʳ Westwood (Trans. Ent. Soc. London V, p. 235, 1850), *A. ichneumoneus* and *A. maculipennis,* can be referred to *Achias* in a very wide sense only.

A. ichneumoneus (East-Indies) does not have the large tegulae of a true *Achias;* its anal cell is slightly drawn out in a point, and not cut off squarely; its whole habitus is entirely different. It may perhaps be referred to the genus *Laglaisia* recently established by M.ʳ Bigot (Ann. Soc. Ent. Fr. 1880, p. 92), for a species from New Guinea.

A. maculipennis from Java belongs again in an entirely different group, as is proved by the absence of the large tegulae, the peculiar venation, and the arrangement of a number of characteristic bristles on the head and the thorax. I look upon it as belonging to the *Trypetidae,* perhaps to *Acanthoneura* Macq.

The data, contained in Wiedemann's paper on *Achias* enable

us to recognize that, in its generic characters, *A. oculatus* coincides, not with the above-mentioned two species, but with the species collected by M.ʳ Wallace in New Guinea and the adjacent islands. The large tegulae and the square distal end of the anal cell, taken in connection with the general habitus and coloring of *A. oculatus* render this conclusion certain, and even lead me to suppose, as I will show below, that *A. oculatus* may be identical with one of M.ʳ Wallace's species. The statement in Wiedemann's essay (p. 13), that the arista is glabrous, is erroneous, and without any foundation, because *Latreille* in his communication about the type of *Fabricius* explicitly says that the arista is broken off (p. 14).

The species of *Achias* were found, as M.ʳ D'Albertis told me, on human alvine dejections.

While at work in the Brit. Mus. in July 1880, I drew up for my own use the following tabular arrangement of the species which may be considered as belonging to *Achias,* in the sense of Wiedemann. Imperfect and hastily put together as it is, it may be of some use to others; I have added my own *A. Albertisii* to it, which, after a good deal of hesitation, I concluded to consider as distinct from *A. longividens.*

Costa not darker colored — **venustula** Walk. J. Pr. Lin. Soc. VIII, 119 (New Guinea).

Costa darker colored
    Femora yellow.

        Stout species — **amplividens** Walk. l. c. III, 122 (Aru Isl.ᵈˢ) and Westwood, Tr. Ent. Soc. N. S. V. Tab. 13, f. 7.
        brachyophthalma Walk. l. c. VIII, 119 (New Guinea).

      Narrow, elongated species — **dacoides** Walk. l. c. VIII, 133 (Salwatti) ♀.
        (Syn. ♂ *aspiciens* Wk. l. c. VII, 229 ♂ Waigiou).

    Femora broadly black at tip — **longividens** Walk. l. c. III, 121 (Aru) and Westwood, l. c.
        latividens Walk. l. c. III, 121 (Aru) and Westwood, l. c.
        Albertisi n. sp. (N. Guinea).

Thus we have seven species (or six if *longividens* and *latividens* be considered as one) all from New Guinea and the
surrounding islands. This geographical distribution of the group
makes it almost certain that the original *Achias oculatus* Fab.
never had Java for its patria, but came from N. Guinea, or still
more probably, from the Aru Islands, whence, for centuries
past, birds of paradise have been exported. If *A. oculatus* really
occurs in Java, it is difficult to explain why it has never been
brought to Europe since? Once being granted that *A. oculatus*
comes from the same region as the six species enumerated
above, it becomes exceedingly probable that it is synonymous
with one of them. As far as the data go, which we possess
about *A. oculatus* (brown costal border and altogether yellow
femora), *A. amplividens* from the Aru Islands comes nearest to
it. Only the specimens of *amplividens* in the Brit. Mus. have a
much narrower head than that of *A. oculatus*, as shown in the
figure.

A few words about the systematic position of *Achias*. I believe it to be an *Ortalid*, related to *Lamprogaster*, which also
have very large tegulae (like a number of other *Platystomina*).
The *Ortalidae* contain several genera with a laterally very developed head; but it does not follow that these broad-headed
genera all belong in the same group. Wiedemann went too far
when he formed a family *Achiidae* for *Achias*, *Plagiocephalus*
and *Zygothrica*, because they are all broad-headed. *Plagiocephalus*, as Loew suspects (Mon. N. Am. Dipt. III, 26)
may belong to the *Richardina*, a group in which Gerstaecker
described two very broad-headed *Richardiae* (Stett. Ent. Zeit.
1860). *Zygothrica*, to all appearances, is no *Ortalid* at all; a
specimen which I saw in Vienna Museum made on me the im-
pression of a *Drosophila*; and I found since a passage of Loew's,
who reached the same conclusion (Monogr. N. Am. Dipt. III,
24); a passage which I had lost sight of since I translated that
volume.

Scholastes cinctus Guérin (*Platystoma*), Voy. Coquille, Zool. 299, Tab. 21, f. 9. (Port Jackson).

SYN. **Acinia faciestriata** Dol. 2de Bijdr. 40, Tab. X, f. 7 (Amboina)!
   Lamprogaster transversa Walk., J. Pr. Lin. Soc. I, 30 (Malacca)!
   »   »   **marginifora** Walk., J. Pr. Lin. Soc. III, 111 (Aru, Batchian, New Guinea).
   »   »   **sexvittata** Walk., J. Pr. Lin. Soc. V, 261 (Celebes)!

Guérin's description is bad, and there must be some clerical error in that of the face ; nevertheless there can be no doubt that it is the same species; Schiner, Novara, 284, also recognizes the identity. I have seen numerous types of Doleschall's in Vienna, and those of Walker in London. Loew (Monogr. etc. III, 38) proposes for this species the genus *Scholastes*.

There are nine ♂ and 12 ♀ specimens in the collection, most of them from Ternate, six from the Aru Islands (Wokan), one from Celebes, two from Amboina ; all collected by M.ʳ Beccari. This seems to be a common species, of wide distribution, as it occurs from Sydney in the South, to the Philippine Islands in the North.

Adrama selecta Walk. J. Pr. Lin. Soc. III, 117 (Aru Isl.^{ds})!

SYN. **Enicoptera rufiventris** Walk. l. c, V, 163 (Amboina)!
   Psila cruciata Walk. l. c. VIII, 126 (New Guinea)!

One ♂, Wokan (Aru Isl.^{ds}), (*Beccari*, 1873).

NB. To the genus *Adrama* Wk. belongs, besides *A. selecta*, a second species, the *Dacus determinatus* Wk. (J. Pr. Lin. Soc. I, 133! Borneo). It is the same as *Acanthipeza maculifrons* Rondani (Ann. Mus. Civ. Genova, VII, p. 438; a female, Borneo!). It is very like *A. selecta*, but is easily distinguished by the color of the upper part of the thorax and that of the scutellum ; the latter is yellow, with a well-marked large black triangle in the middle. I also have a male *A. determinata* from the Philippine Islands. These three specimens enable me to draw the following description of the characters of the genus.

Adrama (Syn. *Acanthipeza* Rond.) has the elongated, smooth body of a *Psila*, or *Loxocera;* it also resembles these genera in the character of its coloring. *Face* moderately excavated: *antennal furrows* diverging, placed near the eyes; cheeks narrow; third antennal joint about 3 times longer than broad, with nearly parallel sides, rounded at tip; arista short-feathery· Ocelli distinct, placed on the vertex. The cephalic bristles are as follows: one each side near the upper corners of the eyes (in the ♀ I perceive a smaller bristle, behind them, on the occiput); a pair of much weaker bristles, one each side, lower down on the front, near the orbit; a pair of minute bristles on each side of the black frontal spot, not far above the antennae. Palpi broad, spatulate. *Thoracic furrow* crossing the thorax, from one side to the other. The *thoracic bristles* are but few; I perceive (in the ♂) one each side back of the humeral callosity; another at each end of the thoracic furrow; and three each side between the furrow and the scutellum; on the pleurae, a very weak bristle is visible a little in front of the root of the wings. *Scutellum* triangular with four bristles. *Abdomen* (4-jointed in the ♂, 5-jointed in the ♀) elongate, attenuated anteriorly, without being pedicelled (not unlike the abdomen of an *Ichneumon*); the first joint nearly as long as the three following taken together (two joints must be soldered together here; the suture is distinct on the ventral side); the three following joints, in the ♂, are of nearly equal length; in the ♀ they gradually diminish in length. *Hypopygium* of the male small, bent under the abdomen. *Ovipositor* of the female funnel-shaped; (in the specimen which I examined, the two inner joints were exerted, so that the whole ovipositor was as long as the abdomen). The middle pair of *legs* is the longest and strongest. All the *femora* have short, stiff bristles on the underside on the distal half, but they are more numerous on the middle pair; (on the front femora of *A. determinata* ♂ ♀, I perceive but one minute spine; in the ♂ of *A. selecta,* two; the numbers may however be variable, especially on the hind and middle femora). The venation is normal. The auxiliary vein is closely approximated to the first vein; it stops abruptly upon reaching the stigma and its connection with the costa is indistinct, coinciding with the edge of the stigma. The crossveins (in both species) run parallel to each other; their distance is a trifle longer than the great crossvein. The second posterior cell is longer than the anal: the latter is drawn out in a point. The hairs on the costa and on the first vein are very minute; those on the beginning of the third vein require a very strong lens.

The Psila-like appearance, the spinose femora and the larger size of the middle pair of legs, render this genus easily recognizable. *Meracantha* Macq. (D. E. Suppl. IV, 285, Tab. 26, f. 9) also has spinose femora, but the hind pair are incrassate, the abdomen clavate, the antennae elongate etc.

Sophira distorta Walk. Trans. Ent. Soc. IV, N. S. pt. VI, 230 ! (Celebes).

SYN. **Enicoptera pictipennis** Walk. J. Pr. Lin. Soc. IV, 155 and V, 262 ! (Celebes).

The descriptions are unrecognizable, but I have seen the types. I do not give any further details about the genus *Sophira*, because I have only a single female before me; besides, I am in doubt whether this species is congeneric with *Sophira venusta* Wk., which I do not know.

Polyara insolita Walk. J. Pr. Lin. Soc. III, 122 ! (Aru Isl.[ds]) *male*, and VII, 221 (Mysol) *female*.

Three specimens (one of them a male; the abdomen of the two others is broken).

Ramoi and Dorei Hum, N. Guinea, Febr. 1875 (*Beccari*).

These flies have very much the appearance of *Tetanocerae*; they can easily be recognized by the abnormal crossveins, which they possess; one in the marginal cell, a little before the end of the first vein; and two in the submarginal cell, dividing it in three section. The female, has an ovipositor as long as the rest of the body.

Anguitula cyanea Guérin (*Nerius*) Voy. de la Coquille, Zool. 301, Tab. 21, f. 11 (Dorei, N. Guin.).

SYN. **Elaphomyia polita** Saund. Tr. Ent. Soc. Lond. V, N. S. 416, Tab. 12, 6
and 13, 1.
Anguitula longicollis Walk. J. Pr. Lin. Soc. III, 123 and V, 297; the
synonymy with *E. polita* is acknowledged
l. c. VII. 222 (Aru, Mysol, Ceram, Salwatti,
Batchian, Gilolo).

Five ♂, three ♀; Andai and Fly River, N. Guinea (*L. M. D'Albertis*): Dorei Hum (*Beccari*).

NB. Anguitula is not unlike a large *Sepsis*, in general appearance, but has several peculiarities, not mentioned in Mr Walker's description.

Venation. The first vein runs so near the costa, that it is discernible with some difficulty, especially beyond the origin of the third vein, where first vein and costa are in close contact; the second vein also runs closely along the first, as far as the origin of the third vein; beyond it, there is a very narrow interval between the first and second veins, which represents the marginal cell. Second basal and anal cells long, but narrow; the anal cell is square at the end, and not drawn out in a point.

The *head* is rounded, the occiput not being distinctly separated from the front and vertex, but strongly projecting and forming a smooth slope, which meets the long thoracic collum. The lower half of the face projects obliquely, at an angle of 45°, forming a smooth slope; but this projection is solid underneath and does not correspond to a proportionate enlargement of the oral opening. Proboscis stout, palpi slender. The antennal foveae are far apart, on both sides of this projection, near the orbits. The third antennal joint is three times longer than broad; the arista hairy on both sides. Cheeks very narrow. No bristles at all on the head; the usual erect bristles on the vertex are replaced by a few hairs, visible only under a strong lens; a row of small bristlets on the cervix, above the junction with the collum.

Thorax smooth, withouth bristles; scutellum with two spines; metanotum large, convex, coalescent with the lateral callosities, which are separated by indistinct sutures only.

Abdomen petiolate, club-shaped; first segment long, petiolate, bell-shaped at the end; the petiole bears two knots; the first, near the root, has a sharp point on each side; the second, in the middle of the segment, forms a transverse ridge. The abdomen of the female has only four joints before the ovipositor; the latter is flat, not longer than the preceding segment. *Hypopygium* of the male small, bent under the abdomen.

Legs moderately long and rather slender, without any spines or bristles; middle tibiae with a short spur; the hind tibiae have a weak and indistinct one.

Judging from Macquart's description of his genus *Omalocephala* (D. R. II, 3, 231), which he refers to the *Sepsidae*, it has a good deal in common with *Anguitula*. It differs in the structure of head and front, of the abdomen, which is said to have seven segments; the scutellum is without spines etc. Loew Monogr. III, 21 and 23 refers it to the *Ortalidae*.

Phytalmia cervicornis Gerstaecker, Stett. Ent. Z. 1860, 173, Tab. 2, f. 4. (New Guinea).

SYN. Elaphomyia cervicornis Saund. V, oct. 1861, N. S. pt. X, Tab. 12, f. 4-5.

Occurs, as M.ʳ Beccari told me, in woods, on the trunks of trees.

14 ♂, 6 ♀ specim. from Ramoi, N. Guinea, June 1872 (*L. M. D'Albertis*); Febr. 1875 (*Beccari*); Andai, N. Guinea, August (*L. M. D'Albertis*).

NB. D.ʳ Gerstaecker's *Phytalmia* being earlier in date has the priority over *Elaphomyia* Saund. The spines on the underside of the front femora exist in the male only.

Of the five species, described by M.ʳ Saunders, only three are really *Elaphomyiae;* the *Elaphomyia brevicornis* is a compound of two species, for which I propose the genus *Diplochorda*. *E. polita* (described much earlier, under another name, by Guérin) may remain in the genus *Anguitula,* introduced by M.ʳ Walker.

484 R. OSTEN SACKEN

Diplochorda, nov. gen.

Elaphomyia brevicornis, ♂ and ♀, described by M.ʳ Saunders in the Trans. Ent. Soc. N. S. V, 415, Tab. 13, f. 2 and 3, represents, I am convinced, two distinct species. The subject of fig. 3 was erroneously taken for the female; the specimen is a male and a different species. If it had been a female, it would have had a long ovipositor, like the other females of *Elaphomyia* (Syn. *Phytalmia* Gerst.) and it would not have the large expansion of the costal margin that, as I learn from specimens in my possession, only belongs to the males. I have before me a male specimen from New Guinea, which answers exactly fig. 3 and the description belonging thereto. This same species was described by M.ʳ Walker as *Dacus turgidus* and I therefore adopt this name for it. I have moreover, from the same country, two females, belonging to the same genus, but to two different, and apparently new, species. For these three species, together with the original *Elaphom. brevicornis* Saund. (l. c. fig. 2), as a fourth, I propose the establishment of the new genus *Diplochorda,* the name of which is derived from its most striking character, the close approximation of the first and second longitudinal veins.

The venation alone is sufficient to characterize it. Its peculiarity consists especially in the coarctation of the marginal and submarginal cells, and a corresponding expansion of the costal, first basal and discal. This character exists in both sexes, but is particularly striking in the male. In *D. turgida* ♂ (the only male I have), the costa is very stout and is bent almost at an angle (see l. c. fig. 3); the auxiliary vein is short, and reaches very little beyond the tip of the anal cell; the first longitudinal vein is unusually stout, like a costa, and ends not very far from the apex of the wing; the costal cell is very broad (at its broadest place it is but little narrower than the length of the anterior crossvein); the second vein runs so close alongside the first, that the marginal cell becomes linear, some attention is required to discern it; the third vein likewise runs alongside of the second and diverges only towards its end; thus the submarginal cell, linear in its proximal portion, becomes trumpet-shaped towards the end. The anterior crossvein is unusually long (as long as the posterior one), which gives an extraordinary breadth to the first basal and first posterior cells; the latter thus appears rather short, and out of shape. The peculiar shape of the discal cell is due to the position of the anterior crossvein, very near its end; to the curvature of the fourth vein, enlarging the first basal cell at the expense of the discal, but, more than all, to the very oblique course of the posterior crossvein, which appears like a prolongation of the fifth vein, and reduces the second posterior cell to a narrow stripe along the margin of the wing. The third posterior cell is likewise narrow, as well as the axillary. The anal cell resembles that of *Phytalmia,* it is small, and drawn out in a short point. The male of *D. brevicornis,* as represented in the Tr. Ent. Soc. l. c. fig. 2 shows, with slight modifications in degree, exactly the same characters.

In the females, the same characteristics exist, only in a lesser degree. The costa is not angularly bent, and thus the wing has the normal shape; the distance between the tips of the auxiliary and of the first vein is very considerable still and the costal cell rather broad (much narrower in *D. ophion* than in *D. myrmex*); the close approximation of the first, second and third veins is the same, (the third vein is a little more distant in *D. myrmex* than in *D. ophion*); the length of the anterior crossvein, the curvature of the antepenultimate section of the fourth vein, and the other parts of the venation are the same as in the male; the posterior crossvein is somewhat less oblique.

The affinity to *Phytalmia* appears especially in the structure of the parts of the head and of the abdomen. The eyes are less rounded, more oval, than in *Phytalmia;* the cheeks less broad. The part of the cheek, under the eye, which in *Phytalmia* ♂ bears the hornlike processes, and in the ♀ is marked by a ridge, descending from the eye downwards, has a similar

ridge here, in both sexes; in *D. brevicornis* ♂ it is developed
into a small hornlike appendage (see Trans. Ent. Soc. 1. c.
fig. 2); in *D. turgida* it is much smaller; still smaller in the
females. The very small and closely approximated ocelli are
placed (as in *Phytalmia*) on the top of the vertex; besides the
two erect bristles behind them, there is another bristle, some
distance in front, on each side near the orbit, which does not
exist in *Phytalmia;* still lower down, not far from the orbit, a
little above the antennae, there is, on each side, a minute erect
bristle (sometimes two), which also exists in the other genus.
The antennae are like those of *Phytalmia;* the arista is likewise
feathery on one side only. The minute fringe of hairs, described
by D.ʳ Gerstaecker as existing on the underside of the second
joint in *Ph.*, I do not perceive here. The occiput is less deve-
veloped and as the anterior part of thorax is less prolonged,
than in *Ph.*, the connection between head and thorax looks more
close, less necklike. The thorax is more rounded and compact ;
its structure, in the main is the same : the part of the metathorax between the foot of the halteres and the root of the
wings is more swollen. The metathorax is very flat and vertical. The structure of the legs is the same, only they are less
long and a little stronger : the front femora have a single spine
on the underside in the ♂ (two or three in *Ph.*), none in the
♀. The abdomen of the ♂ has four, that of the ♀ five segments; the first segment (petiole), is shorter than in *Ph.;* the
ovipositor is about $^2/_3$ of the abdomen in length, in the shape
of a narrow funnel (convex above and below, and gradually
attenuated towards the tip.

It is not easy to assign to *Phytalmia* and *Diplochorda* a fit-
ting position in the system, as it exists at present. Gerstaecker,
in describing it among a number of *Ortalidae*, seems to assume
its membership in that polymorphous family. At least Loew
takes it so (Monogr. N. Am. Dipt. III, 27) when he quotes
Phytalmia among the Ortalideous genera, introduced by Gerstaecker. But neither of these authors discusses the question
further. The structure of the funnelshaped ovipositor of the two

genera in question is certainly not that of an Ortalid. If therefore they are admitted into that family, they will have to form a group for themselves, like *Pyrgota,* which also has a peculiar ovipositor. In other respects, the characters of the *Ortalidae,* as given by Loew, l. c. p. 28-31, are well applicable to *Phytalmia* and *Diplochorda.* In my specimen of *D. turgida* male, the long, tape-like penis, rolled up in a spiral, which characterizes the *Ortalidae,* is exerted, and distinctly visible.

The four species of *Diplochorda,* mentioned by me, may be tabulated as follows:

I. The brown color of the apex of the wings does not reach and cover the crossveins.
    Prevailing color of the abdomen brown, only a yellow crossband on the first segment.
        Thorax black . . . . *brevicornis* Saund.
        Thorax with yellow stripes . . . . *turgida* Walk.
        Prevailing color of the abdomen yellow . . . *ophion* n. sp.
II. The brown color of the apex of the wings covers the anterior and a portion of the posterior crossveins . . *myrmex* n. sp.

Diplochorda turgida Walk. (*Dacus*) J. Pr. Lin. Soc. VIII, 134! (Salwatti).

SYN. **Elaphomyia brevicornis** Saund. (ex parte) Trans. Ent. Soc. Lond.
V, N. S. pt. X, Oct. 1861, 415, Tab. 13.
fig. 3 (Dorei, New Guinea).
Dacus concisus Walk. J. Pr. Lin. Soc. V, 252! (Dorei, N. Guin.).

One male; Ramoi, N. Guinea, June 1872 (*L. M. D'Albertis*). I have already said above, that *Elaphomyia brevicornis* ♀ described and figured by Saunders, l. c. (fig. 3, *not* f. 2), cannot be a female, because the figure does not show the ovipositor, and the wings are represented with the characteristic dilatation of the male. It is therefore a different species and coincides with the *Dacus turgidus* Walk. *Dacus concisus* Walk. seems to be the female of this species; the descriptions of both agree quite well; I also had a glimpse of the types in the British Museum.

Diplochorda ophion n. sp. ♀.

Head, antennae and palpi yellow: arista black; a double, brown spot on the front, about midway between antennae and ocelli. Thorax yellow; a narrow brown line in the middle of the dorsum, interrupted anteriorly before the collare; the suture, on each side, is tinged with brown, which color expands into a larger spot, about midway between the root of the wings and the humerus; a brown streak between this spot and a smaller dot in front of the humerus; an oblique brown streak in the middle of the pleurae and a brown shadow above the posterior coxae. Abdomen black, as far as the middle of the first segment; yellow beyond, with two large, osculant black spots, occupying (one each side), the end of the first and the sides of the 2^d and 3^d segments. Ovipositor ferruginous-yellow, a little longer than the four last segments taken together. Halteres yellow; legs yellow, femora with faint vestiges of a brownish ring; front coxae brownish; tarsi brownish, hind metatarsus yellowish. Wings subhyaline; costal border, inside of the third vein, brown; near the apex this color crosses that vein, encroaching a little upon the first post. c.; an irregular brown cloud along the fifth vein, inside of the third post. c.; it is connected with the brown on the costa, across the crossveins closing the basal cells. Length: 6-7 mm. (without the ovipositor).

Hab. Hatam, New Guinea, July 1875 (*Beccari*); one female.

NB. The specimen being a female, the costa is not expanded; the venation differs from that of *D. myrmex* ♀ as follows: the first, second and third veins run closer to each other and to the costa, hence, the cells between them are narrower; the last section of the third vein is more curved; the antepenultimate section of the fourth vein less curved, than in *myrmex;* the anal cell less drawn out in a point; the posterior crossvein more straight.

Diplochorda myrmex n. sp. ♀.

Head yellow; third joint of the antennae brownish, arista black; a triangular brown spot on the face, at each end of the antennal furrows; a double brown spot on the front, about midway between antennae and ocelli; a smaller spot on each side, above, near the orbit; ocelli on black ground; three brown shadows on the occiput. Ground color of thorax yellow, with many black stripes and spots: three such stripes on the dorsum, all three interrupted in the region of the thoracic suture, but continued again beyond it; only the middle one, attenuated, reaches the reddish-yellow scutellum; metathorax with two black stripes; pleurae mostly black; the yellow portions are: a streak above the front coxae, connected with a large spot in front of the root of the wings; another streak above the middle coxae, not reaching the root of the wings; a large spot between the halteres and the root of the wings. Halteres yellow. Abdomen black; a yellow crossband in the middle of the first segment; fifth segment and hind margin of the fourth, reddish; ovipositor ferruginous, equal in length to two thirds of the abdomen. Front legs: coxae blackish, femora yellow, with a brown ring; tibiae brown; tarsi black; middle legs brown, the femora being broadly yellow at base; hind legs darker brown, especially the tibiae: the femora yellow at base. Wings hyaline; a brown costal border, inside of the second vein; a small hyaline space between the costa and the auxiliary vein; apex of the wings brown, the boundary of this color running parallel to, and not far from, the anterior crossvein, on its proximal side, and then obliquely towards the hind margin, which it reaches near the end of the fifth vein, inside of the second post. cell; a brown band runs along the fifth vein, becomes broader on the crossveins, closing the basal cells, and thus reaches the costal border; it also emits a branch running along the tip of the anal cell, and the sixth vein. Length: about 9 mm., without the ovipositor.

Hab. Katau, N. Guinea (*L. M. D'Albertis*); one female.

NB. The posterior crossvein is a little arcuated; the antepenultimate section of the fourth vein very much so, towards its tip, giving the first basal cell an almost club-shaped appearance. A detailed comparison between the venation of *D. ophion* and *myrmex* has been given above.

Diopsis attenuata Dolesch. I Bijdr. 413, Tab. 8, f. 2. (Java)!

SYN. **Diopsis latimana** Rondani, Ann. Mus. Civ. Genova, VII, 444 (Borneo)!
Diopsis lativola Rondani, ibid.!

One specimen from Buitenzorg, Java (*G. B. Ferrari*, 1875);
Seven specimens from Sumatra; Sungei Bulu, Sept. 1878; Singalang, July 1878: Ajer Mantcior, August 1878 (*Beccari*).
The specimens before me show variations in the coloring, which is more or less reddish or brown; in the length of the oculiferous peduncles, which vary from 6 to 15 mm. from end to end; in the greater or lesser incrassation of the middle tibiae; in the greater or lesser depth of the excision on the fore femora, which, in some specimens, apparently females, is almost obliterated. Nevertheless I hold them all to belong to the same species, for which I adopt the name *attenuata* Dol., as I have seen the type in Vienna. In M.ʳ Rondani's woodcut of the front leg of *latimana* the expanded first tarsal joint is made too short: it should be twice as long as the four remaining joints together. The distinguishing characters of *lativola* Rond. are among the variable ones, and do not, in my opinion, justify a separation.

Diopsis subnotata Westwood, Cabinet of Oriental Entomology, Tab. 18, f. 2. (Philippine Islands)!
The above-quoted figure, at least in the copy which I consulted, is colored too black. I have named my specimens after the type in Oxford, and possess the same species from the Philippine Islands.

Diopsis sp. Mt. Singalang, Sumatra, July 1878 (*Beccari*); a single specimen. It has two pairs of spines on the thorax, besides those on the scutellum, and therefore belongs in the subgenus *Teleopsis* Rond. I cannot identify this species with *T. breviscopium* Rond. which differs in the coloring of the body, legs and wings, and is smaller. *T. breviscopium* Rond. and *longiscopium* Rond., of which I have examined the types, seem to me to be the same species, the differences in the length of the ocular stalks and in the coloring notwithstanding.

Diopsis sp. Java, (*Beccari*, 1875), two specimens. Also a *Teleopsis*, but certainly different from the preceding. The coloration of the wings is exactly like that of *D. attenuata.*

NB. It would be rash to describe the above two species as new, without a critical revision of all the asiatic species of *Diopsis,* that, from want of material, I am unable to attempt. But what I have seen in the collections which I have visited has convinced me, that the species have been unnecessarily multiplied. Some 14 or 15 species of *Diopsis* from the Eastern Archipelago have been described, belonging in the group with banded wings, besides four or five from other parts of southern Asia; two species from those regions are known, which have a single apical spot; and only one (*D. Hearseyana* Westw.) with colorless wings; twenty three asiatic species in all.

Celyphus obtectus (Dalman) Wied. Auss. Zw. II, 601 (East-Indies).

A dozen specimens from Buitenzorg, Java (*G. B. Ferrari* 1875) and from Singapore.

The Brit. Mus. possesses specimens from the Philippines, Hong Kong and Calcutta. ·

Celyphus scutatus Wied. Auss. Zw. II, 601 (East-Indies).

One specimen from Buitenzorg (Java), *G. B. Ferrari.*

Celyphus levis v. d. Wulp, MSS. (Sumatra).

Two specimens from Ajer Mantcior, Sumatra (*Beccari*, Aug. 1878). It resembles a specimen labelled *C. fuscipes* Macq. sent by M.ʳ Bigot to the Museum in Vienna, but is much smoother (less punctate) and more shining. I prefer to use the name under which M.ʳ v. d. Wulp intends to describe it in a forthcoming paper on the diptera of Sumatra.

Notiphila sinensis Schiner, Novara etc. 241 (Hong Kong)!
Four specimens; Kandari, Celebes, April 1874 (*Beccari*).
The description agrees sufficiently well to render the identification very little doubtful.

Notiphila sp. Two specimens, Has, N. Guinea, Febr. 1875 (*Beccari*).

Sepsis testacea Walk. J. Pr. Lin. Soc. IV, 163.
Three specimens, Kandari, Celebes, Apr. 1874 (*Beccari*).

Observation. Besides the enumerated species, the collection contains five species of *Sapromyza* from Celebes, New Guinea and the Aru Islands, an *Eurina* from Celebes, one or two other *Chloropids* (N. Guinea, Aru Isl.[ds]), a *Piophilid* (Celebes), a *Phora* (Sumatra) and some species of doubtful systematic position.

For the sake of completeness, I add the following list of the *Pupipara*, from the same collections of M.ʳ O. Beccari and others, extracted from Prof. Rondani's paper on that family:

Nycteribia Albertisi Rond. Ann. Mus. Civ. Gen. XIII, p. 150.
Ins. Goram.
» **Jenynsi** (West.) Rond. l. c. 151. Amboina.

Myiophthiria reduvioides Rond. l. c. 154. Borneo (*Beccari*).
» **lygaeoides** Rond. l. c. 155. Amboina (*id.*).

Ornithomyia andajensis Rond. l. c. 155. Andai, N. Guin. (*id.*).
» **Batchiana** Rond. l. c. 158. Grafton, Australia (*L. M. D'Albertis*).
» **hatamensis** Rond. l. c. 158. Hatam, N. Guinea (*Beccari*).

Ornithoica Beccariina Rond. l. c. 160. Amboina (*id.*).

Olfersia papuana Rond. l. c. 163. Hatam, N. Guin. (*id.*).

Brachytarsina amboinensis Rond. l. c. 166, Amboina (*id.*).

www.ingramcontent.com/pod-product-compliance
Lightning Source LLC
Chambersburg PA
CBHW030837300326
41935CB00037B/584